LIFE
IS NOT A
SPECTATOR
SPORT

BOB COX

iUniverse

LIFE IS NOT A SPECTATOR SPORT

iUniverse books may be ordered through booksellers or by contacting:

iUniverse
1663 Liberty Drive
Bloomington, IN 47403
www.iuniverse.com
844-349-9409

Because of the dynamic nature of the Internet, any web addresses or links contained in this book may have changed since publication and may no longer be valid. The views expressed in this work are solely those of the author and do not necessarily reflect the views of the publisher, and the publisher hereby disclaims any responsibility for them.

Any people depicted in stock imagery provided by Getty Images are models, and such images are being used for illustrative purposes only.
Certain stock imagery © Getty Images.

ISBN: 978-1-6632-0692-3 (sc)
ISBN: 978-1-6632-0693-0 (e)

Print information available on the last page.

iUniverse rev. date: 08/27/2020

Contents

Foreword

Why write a book about the life of an ordinary guy?

For starters, maybe it's not an ordinary life.

I boot-strapped myself from a background that would at best be called lower middle class, succeeding in careers as a sports writer, and later as a teacher and school administrator. When it was done, I was Superintendent of a small school district in Southern California on an interim basis for one year after seven years as an assistant superintendent.

I went head-to-head with an affinity for alcohol that was certainly a full-fledged addiction at the age of 45, and I have survived a serious cancer of the throat, as well as multiple skin cancers, and few other health challenges.,

At 72, as I am publishing these memoirs, I have outlived my parents and most of my relatives. Many friends who had meaningful impact on my life are no longer around.

But I'm at the gym nearly every morning at 5 a.m., riding the exercise bike, logging miles on the treadmill, or tossing around a few pounds of metal.

This has been a life lived with one motivating motto:

Life is Not a Spectator Sport.

In living this life through 72 years, I have taken chances, been lucky, been unlucky, made mistakes, stubbed my toes, broken a few bones, and survived challenges both manmade and tossed my way by life.

This memoir touches on some of the milestones that have shaped my life. The focus is on events early more than later, since the intended audience knows quite a bit about the last 25 years.

In getting to know on an adult level, my three children, Lisa Bulsombut, Randy Cox and Allie Cox, I've come to realize they all know chapters and vignettes of my life, but few can weave the full story together. Similarly, my wife and soulmate of 35 years as well as the mother of Randy and Allie, Nancy, knows only what she has heard about the first 38 years.

Others know bits and pieces. Few know more than a sprinkling.

Although I have been there for many major events, including one Olympic Games, 19 Super Bowls, a handful of World Series, and a few other high-profile events, this is not about those games. If you want to read about the Raiders' Super Bowl win after the 1983 season, there are better resources. This is not the sports writer's career highlights book, but rather a recounting of one man's life.

There are tidbits about a few unusual assignments, and the journalism thread works its way throughout the narrative, but that is not the theme. Rather, this is a presentation of my world for the edification of my kids.

As a promise to Randy and Allie, I have chosen to tell my tales in a book which is not intended for the commercial market, although it may be available for purchase.

I am attempting to stick to chronological order, since in reading the books of colleagues, those who jumped out of order consistently made it tougher on the reader. There is no journalistic inverted pyramid here. No consistent hierarchy of events. You may find a nugget among the minutia, in other words.

Perhaps a few facts have been polished by time. Perhaps the memories are so good because they, too, have benefitted from the softening of the ages. Fact checking is unavailable, so you'll have to take facts at face value, or for what I say they are worth.

I've tried not to rely on the adage that you never let a fact stand in the way of a good story.

The facts are what they are, as I believe them. And I have no resource other than my own memory to confirm a street fight between two bar hostesses in Sagami-Otsuka, Japan, in the fall of 1968. What you get from me is the only version that exists, to my knowledge. There were no published news accounts of this minor moment in history.

Similarly, so many of the events that shaped my life exist only as memories, perhaps accurate, perhaps not.

But these are the moments that add up to the final product for me.

I am telling this story for my children, my wife, my friends, and anybody else that cares. And I have tried to stick to the basic theme of my life:

Life Is Not A Spectator Sport

Bob Cox
Summer 2020

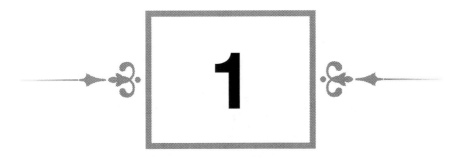

THE EARLY YEARS IN SANTA MONICA (1947 TO 1959)

I have no memories of being born at Santa Monica Hospital, other than the fact it was only two blocks from our extremely modest two-bedroom apartment at 1623 Arizona Avenue. Our four-apartment building was torn down for a medical building in the 1960s.

I also learned that my birthday, Dec. 30, was considered a windfall for my parents on their tax return. It took me until my 20s before I understood why that mattered. My brother, on the other hand, arrived on Jan. 4, 1949, so my parents paid full price for that tax deduction with a full year's worth of expenses.

Most of my memories of the early years are of my brother Ronnie and me together, or with our parents.

Dad worked as a furniture salesman at Coast Furniture on 4th Street in Santa Monica. Mom worked as a beautician when we were toddlers. She became a stay-at-home mom by the time we went to school. This may have been because of the crippling arthritis in her hands, or for other reasons. Parents didn't talk much to kids about decisions in those days. Things were just the way they were. No meaningful dialogue or explanations.

I remember that Mimmie, my mother's mother, Mildred Krause, lived in the apartment above us. This was my haven in those days. If I got in trouble with the parents, I could flee to Mimmie's for a while, and things would be better.

My cousin Paula later explained the dynamic: She was Mimmie's favorite among her three sisters, and I was the favorite among our two brothers. Seven years older than me, Paula helped me understand how that worked when we reconnected later in life. But for most of my early years, I just enjoyed without question the most favored position.

Our family consisted of Kenneth William Cox, born July 18, 1906 in Aurora, Nebraska, and Lorena Bernell Walker Cox, born Nov. 30, 1919 in Santa Monica. It was the second marriage for both, although they rarely talked about their first marriages to Ronnie and I. Kenny and Rena were married in March 1947, so I was just legal in the nine-month parameter of that era when married status was important to the offspring.

Dad was the parent of two children (Bill and Shirley) in his previous marriage, and Bill had two kids that were about our age. We saw them occasionally and marveled that we were uncles to them, even though we were within a few years in age. I have no memories of Shirley's family.

Later, when my own life was shaping up and I started a family with Nancy, I realized that I was repeating many of the steps of my father: This was my second marriage, our first child was born when I was 42 (if only for two more days) and we gave the kid a Christmas birthday. Funny how even family history repeats itself. There must be a lesson there.

I remember playing Little League baseball for a dreadfully named team called the Hoot Owls. Who ever wanted to admit he played for the Hoot Owls? Our league named the teams for their sponsors. We were sponsored by the Owl Drug Store. There was a team called the Below Deckers (Below Deck Café at the Santa Monica Pier) and a team called the 7-Uppers (the soft drink). The other teams in the league escape me, but they must have had similarly awful names.

I wasn't very good at baseball to start with, but I had tenacity. I was willing to throw the ball against the wall a thousand times to learn to field ground balls. That didn't help me as a hitter, but I improved as a fielder enough to play 2nd base. About that time, I also read a book called *Little League Catcher,* and decided I wanted to become one. Again, hard work trumped talent, and I became pretty good at this unpopular position. At the end of my 11-year-old season, and before we moved to Idaho, I was an "honorary" all-star. They picked 12 all-stars, and two honorary all-stars. I didn't make the all-star team, but I was close enough for a mention.

All of which would bode well for my 12-year-old season – the year when you become an all-star and make your name as a Little League player. But then we moved to Idaho.

I remember little about school at McKinley Elementary. My memories are about riding bikes, playing baseball or other games, and weekend sports on the wide-open campus. Not much about academics. I can tell you that I had a male teacher in 5th grade. Mr. Tanner. How rare was it to have a male elementary teacher in the 1950s? Mr. Tanner did a couple of things I will always remember: He tried to engage me in conversation about something I cared about, baseball, by asking me a question he probably knew the answer to (Why do they call it the bullpen?). But more importantly, he suggested I learn to type as soon as possible, because my hand-writing was dreadful and barely legible. That was a revelation and I was typing within the next year or so and have not handwritten anything longer than a grocery list for most of my life.

Other memories of the early years include a lot of baseball and other sports. We'd play a form of baseball (with a rubber-coated softer ball) on the playground before school. We'd play at lunch – after scarfing down food in a hurry – and we'd play after school and on weekends. Playgrounds were open to the public, and kids, in those days. There was supervision in the afternoons and sometimes on Saturdays and sometimes in the summer.

Coach Bob Hillen lives on in many of my memories. He was a P.E./Special Ed teacher somewhere in the Santa Monica district, but he also seemed to have all of the cool extra-duty assignments like running the playground on weekends and holidays. He taught me about keeping score in baseball, and he taught us about sportsmanship and the rules of the game. He was a major factor in our young lives. I remember he took a bunch of us to see Santa Monica City College play somebody from the Midwest in the Junior Rose Bowl, a game that was played at the real Rose Bowl in early December involving community college teams. They were called Junior Colleges in those days.

There was also a part-time coach/playground supervisor named A.D. Williams, who I learned had played a couple of seasons in the NFL with the legendary Green Bay Packers. In those days, football players didn't make movie-star salaries and had to work in the off-season. We didn't realize there was an actual NFL player in our midst until years later.

We also played basketball, and football on the playgrounds. Football included Saturday and Sunday pickup football games, 8, 9, 10 or 11 men on a side, full tackle, with no gear. These games were considered plums for we pint-sized elementary kids, because they were dominated by high school and junior high kids. If we got on a team, we were usually nothing but blockers, and we got shoved around a lot. But we loved being included.

One Sunday I slipped on the wet grass, fell backwards, and broke my thumb. Since there were no adults around, and I knew I was in pain, I walked the eight blocks to St. John's Hospital. The nurses tried to contact my parents through the house phone – no cell phones in the 1950s – and I sat for hours while my parents were grocery shopping. I think the nurses gave me some smelling salts to keep me awake. Medical personnel knew I had a broken thumb, but couldn't fix it – or give me pain meds – until my parents arrived.

That was my badge of honor the next day at school since I'd broken my thumb in the football game with the big kids. Never mind that my injury was non-contact related nor sustained making some heroic play.

In the summer after my 6th grade year (schools were K-6 for elementary, 7-9 for junior high and 10-12 for high school in those days), we drove to Idaho to visit my father's sister and her husband, Aunt Hazel and Uncle Carl Larsen, on their small farm outside Nampa.

A few weeks after that rare vacation, my father learned he had an ulcer, and he would be better living a less stressful life. My parents decided to move to Idaho.

I had started at Lincoln Junior High when the decision was made. Starting over in a new city is not ideal for any kid and it probably took me a year to make friends in Nampa. Three years later, we were moving back to Santa Monica.

Idaho was great, for so many things, and it came at the right time for me.

When we returned to Santa Monica, I felt I knew a few things about life. Who else had bucked hay bales onto a moving flat-bed truck? Or picked strawberries? Or sprayed evil weeds in an alfalfa (hay) field? Or started driving a car at the age of 13½, and gotten his license at 14? Or swam in irrigation ditches? Or had his junior high algebra teacher suddenly called out of class because his cows had gotten out of the pasture? But the capper: Who else had 6 pregnancies in a 9th grade graduation class of about 200? That's six percent if you're just counting girls.

THE RURAL LIFE IN IDAHO (1959-62)

When my parents decided to move to Idaho, in October 1959, there was no consultation with Ronnie and me. Kids just went along.

We had enjoyed our week of vacation at Aunt Hazel and Uncle Carl's in the summer – what city kid wouldn't enjoy being on a real farm with haystacks, cows, pigs and chickens? But moving there was another story. No kid handles moving well, and we were certainly not prepared for this. We'd had our friends through six years of school, and knew how to hang out. Sports was an important part of that life.

Now we were uprooted. We lived for a few weeks in sleeping bags on the floor at Hazel and Carl's place. This was while my father searched for work, and we probably lived off the charity of the family. I'm not sure if there was unemployment compensation in Nampa, Idaho, in those days, or even if a guy moving in from California could qualify. Finances were not discussed with kids, other than the routine explanation, "we can't afford that," for almost any purchase.

We moved into a tiny duplex in town. A place that had only one bedroom. Not sure how we managed that through that first winter, but by the spring, my dad had turned the enclosed back porch into a room that became a bedroom for my brother and me. He used some kind of clear plastic to insulate it and used space heaters. That heating and insulation was necessary, since for the first winter, we did not have a refrigerator, and we kept the milk and other cold goods in that unheated porch.

We were slow to make friends. It didn't help that I enrolled in one junior high school for a week while we were still staying on the farm, then transferred to the other school after we got our "house" in town. But sports helped, and I made friends through basketball and football. We also played baseball in a town league that was sort of like Little League. But the teams weren't as well organized as those in Santa Monica, and I sort of drifted away from the game after two seasons.

Because this was gun country, I began reading magazines about hunting, and I became a junior member of the NRA, the National Rifle Association. Ronnie and I got Daisy BB guns – rifles with scopes – for Christmas. I learned that I could take marksmanship tests and win medals. I remember the NRA would mail me paper targets, and I would shoot on a 15-foot range in the garage, then mail the targets back in order to receive my sharpshooter medal. I found a couple of those in a cigar box of long-forgotten treasures not too long ago. Imagine: 60 years ago, I was a sharpshooter with a BB gun.

I also wanted to hunt, because I kept hearing and reading about the glories of hunting. After my constant badgering, my father took me on a few hunts. He'd borrow a couple of rifles, or shotguns, and we'd tramp around the woods for half a day. We chased deer without ever seeing one, or firing that Winchester Model 94 30-30 that I loved to carry. Another time, Dad borrowed a couple of shotguns and we went pheasant hunting. Also, with no success. But I did fire the 12-gauge shotgun at a duck flying overhead. Learned a lot from that shot, by the way. The 12-gauge shotgun kicks mightily, and you don't shoot straight up. The gun knocked me on my 13-year-old ass, seriously bruised my right shoulder, and made me realize I didn't know much about this type of hunting.

Later on, at about 14, I would go rabbit hunting with my friend, Ron Stiles. He had a 22-caliber rifle, and his mother would drive us in their Studebaker out to the desert area near town. She'd drive through the sagebrush at night, with one of us sitting on top of each headlight. When the jackrabbits would stop to stare into the lights, we'd shoot them from about 25 feet away. Hardly sporting, and highly illegal, but we were hunting live game. We'd miss as many as we'd hit, but we did rid the world of a couple of dozen jackrabbits each time we went hunting.

I also remember the freedom Idaho kids had. We'd leave home in the morning on Saturday or during vacations and not come home 'til dinner. There were no cell phones and no way to check in with home. But we never seemed to get in much trouble. We'd ride inner tubes for miles on the irrigation ditches; jump into creeks or ditches off 20-foot rock outcroppings, dare each other to jump a fence into the field where a notorious bull lived, then run like hell to escape when the bull chased us.

We were free to grow up and make mistakes with little adult supervision.

One year for Easter, my parents bought two baby chickens, and my dad built a cage to keep them. After the appropriate amount of feeding and growth, they were suddenly missing and had become a couple of meals.

About that time, on one of our all-day bicycle rides to nowhere, my friends and I wound up at a field near the downtown slaughterhouse. A few of the thousands of chickens being loaded from a truck to their ultimate fate got away. My friends and I realized what great sport it was to chase and capture wild chickens. We'd stuff them in a burlap sack and bring them home. Mom and Dad would feed the next batch of chickens, which would then feed us.

Then we got impatient one day when there weren't any runaway chickens in the lot, and we figured out how easy it was to liberate the chickens from the truck … and help them gain a little freedom in our burlap sacks.

I'm not sure how many chickens wound up as part of the Cox family food bank, but it was probably more than a couple. Were we doing anything illegal? Grand theft chicken? These chickens were paroled minutes before being attached to the conveyer belt of death, and got a few weeks more of life.

Winter brought an appreciation for a particularly sporting game called Hooky-Bobbing. It's a game that probably lasted for decades, but modern cars have meant the demise of hooky-bobbing. With snow on the ground, preferably several inches, kids would run out behind moving cars, grab on to the rear bumper, and remaining in a catcher-like squatting position, ride around behind the car for as long as you dared. Or until you were soaking wet, or had muscle fatigue, or had worn out the bottoms of your shoes or boots.

Hooky-bobbing was illegal, just a little dangerous, and great fun. The joy in catching on behind a driver who did not know you were there was part of the sport. But it was even more challenging when a young adult, or teenager, knew you were behind and did everything he could to throw you off by hitting bumps, or puddles, or manhole covers, or making swerving turns. Our parents warned us repeatedly about the dangers or this, but no kid to my knowledge was ever seriously injured doing it,

Cars were moving to sleeker, tougher-to-grab bumpers in the 1960s, and I'm sure more modern cars have rendered the sport extinct now. Bumpers? What's a bumper?

I also had my first jobs in Idaho. Picking strawberries seemed like the best of all worlds. You had to be 13 (not sure why), and boys and girls would all sign up. They'd bus a bunch of us to a field, turn us loose with a tray, and we'd work from 6 a.m. 'til early afternoon. The pay was 50 cents for a flat (8 little baskets in the store) of berries. You had to pick a minimum of 3 flats to get invited back for the next day. Because most of us alternated eating a strawberry, then putting one in the basket, then throwing a third at our friend who was several rows over, we barely made the three-flat minimum. $1.50 for 8 hours work. Even in those days the minimum wage was $1 an hour. And we were all so sick of strawberries we didn't eat them again for the rest of the summer.

I later did my turn with a hoe on the sugar beet crops that dominated around Nampa. Another short-term job. But the best job I had was bucking hay bales. My dad somehow hooked me up with a farmer he knew, and this was a coveted job. Usually this was reserved for the high school football players. The farmer would drive a tractor with a flat trailer behind, through the fields where hay had recently been cut and baled by a combine. One kid would be on the flat, stacking the bales. While one kid walked on each side, tossing (or bucking) the bales onto the flat truck. It was hard work and the farmer never slowed the tractor, so you had to keep up.

I learned a lot of lessons my first two days on this job. A hay bale weighs more in the morning when it's wet. Hay bales can cut up your exposed forearms in a nasty way, and you learn to savor your few breaks. The day began right after dawn at 5:30 a.m. and dinner (the mid-day meal on farms) was often served at 10:30 or 11 a.m. The farmer would bring the three kids into the house and his wife would prepare a major meal. After

45 minutes of respite, we'd be back out in the fields to finish the 8-hour shift. This was premium work so it paid more, $1.10 an hour instead of the usual $1.00.

And I was so exhausted after two days of this, I could not even imagine whatever evening activities we had at the age of 14. I lasted two days at bucking hay bales, and that job ended. Not sure if I would have gone back given the chance. I figured I might let the muscle-building football players have the job.

Our family scored another prime farm job through Dad's connections. This was called "spraying dodder," and involved killing the "dodder" weed that strangled and killed alfalfa hay plants.

One person on the three-person crew walked in the middle, carrying the 20-gallon spray can of some toxic weed killer. The two other people spread out several rows to each side and spotted weeds. Normally you'd trade off carrying and spraying with the spotters, but my mom never carried the tank. We three did this for about six weeks in the summer of 1962.

Ronnie and I learned about life in Santa Monica during the war years from my mother on those long days in the hay fields. She lived a pretty good lifestyle, including trips to the mob-owned "Rex" gambling ship, which was anchored outside the legal limit of 3 miles off shore.

Ronnie and I donated part of our earnings to the family coffers so we could return to Santa Monica on vacation later that summer.

Once I learned we were moving back to California in August, I was relieved of the nasty pre-high school project most 9th graders were working on, collecting a couple dozen bugs or insects, for a 10th grade biology project. The Big Board was something I gladly skipped as we reversed our move of three years earlier.

As I reflect on my Idaho experience, it was a major growing period for me. There were about 200 kids in our 9th grade class at West Junior High, and there were six pregnancies. I had nothing to do with the statistic. Farm kids grew up earlier, for starters. And there was a social stigma involved. One of the "cool kids" of the class, Mary Ann Newton – it's amazing how you remember certain names for 60 years – was the daughter of a prominent car dealer and lived in a fancy house. When Mary Ann became impregnated by an older boy, her family sold their car dealership, and their fancy house, and moved to Utah. Guess they were members of one of the many LDS (Mormon) temples in town.

Although the farm labor jobs are the strongest memories, my first job came the spring after we moved to Idaho. I got a paper route, riding my bicycle through rain, sleet, snow and other nasty weather to deliver about 100 copies of the Nampa *Free Press* six afternoons a week. There were no Sunday editions of the *Free Press*. The paper cost $1.50 per month, and the paper boy had to collect and then pay his dealer in the first week or so of each month. You can't imagine how many people would put me off for a day or two for a lousy buck and a half. One thing I learned through that – never make the paper boy come back a second time. And always tip. We rarely got more than a 50-cent tip, but it was coveted.

To get that job, I needed a bicycle. I learned about buying on credit at the age of 12. With my father co-signing, I bought a 20-dollar bike at a store in town and agree to pay $5 per month. That was basically how much I earned each month, so I had to make the collections on time to make my bike payment on time. I think I later bought a pair of football cleats on credit too, maybe $15 total and five bucks a month. So, my earnings from the paper route went to credit payments for the first seven months of my labor.

In addition to Ron Stiles, who was product of a divorced family and lived with his mother, my other best friend in the Idaho years was Steve Miner, son of an Idaho State Patrolman. Mr. Miner kept his Oldsmobile cruiser in the family garage and would go out on patrol for 8 or 10 hours every day. The Miners had three older sons, and Steve was a surprise maybe 10 years younger than his closest sibling. They were more upper middle class, so we always hung out at their house.

Steve was more the golden boy, starring in basketball, and he also had a girlfriend before the rest of us. Patrolman Miner was promoted to sergeant at the end of our 9th grade year, and Steve and family were moving to Pocatello about the time we were moving back to California. I always wondered how he turned out, whether he went on to high school or college stardom in basketball, or whether he went into the family business and became a state patrolman.

Nampa was the fifth largest town in Idaho back then with a population of about 17,000. Now it is probably closer to 100,000. But it definitely created some small-town memories: There was a girl in our class who was apparently available to the cool boys, or those with money, or both. Can't verify whether either was true, since I was neither cool nor moneyed. But everyone knew where Candy lived, and we uncool, unmoneyed kids would hang around the neighborhood at night to find out who came calling on Candy.

There were other activities we could participate in at night, which cost no money and raised only a little trouble. Turning on the irrigation water at someone's house was a good example. People flooded their lawns one night a week through the town's irrigation system. But if we flooded it off schedule, the family would come out to find a lake of 6-inch-deep water on their lawn. Before water shortages, this was considered harmless.

Another prank we enjoyed was filling a brown paper bag with fresh cow manure, then leaving it on the porch of our intended target. One guy would light the bag on fire, while another knocked on the door, then we'd run for cover. The crabby neighbor we were picking on would come out in his boots, or shoes, and stomp out the small fire, only to get his boots covered with very fresh cow manure. Once again, this was mostly harmless.

I did participate in another childhood prank that could easily have been far more harmful, though. Because of the heavy church influence in Nampa in the early 1960s, many businesses were not open on Sundays. Car dealerships were among them.

Ronnie learned that the used car dealers often left keys in some cars over the weekend. He and I and some other kid picked out a shiny 1956 Ford one Sunday morning, and took it for a daylong test drive around the countryside. I was 13½ and had my learner's permit (licenses were issued at 14 in Idaho in those days), and the other two were 12 years old. We probably put 150 miles on that car that day. Remember that gas was only about 25 cents a gallon. Included in those miles was a bit of high-speed experimenting, including one nearly disastrous run across the front lawn of a corner farm. Fortunately, the owners were at church, since it was Sunday morning. Also, fortunately there were no fences or lawn furniture. Also, fortunate I did not run into Patrolman Miner, or any of his colleagues.

We "borrowed" a couple of other cars in the next few weeks. Then we had one old tanker that broke down while we had it off the lot. We left it where it broke down. And I read in the *Free Press* – the paper I delivered and also read – that there was a stolen car reported to police. They eventually found it, but I realized the jump from joy-riding to stealing cars was not a large one. So, I pulled out of the weekend test driving club with no one the wiser. That's a stunt that easily could have gone badly.

Besides, I was getting a lot of chances to drive the family car, a 1955 Chevrolet station wagon, as I was working towards my license. I received it on my birthday, Dec. 30, 1961. I was a licensed driver at the age of 14, although those licenses were restricted to daylight only. You got a full day-and-night license at 16.

When we returned to Santa Monica, I had that Idaho license, but someone told my parents it was not valid in California. My parents mostly adhered to that, except when they needed me to drive to the store and pick up something.

A few more random memories of the early 1960s in Nampa:

- Dad had to drive about 10 miles to the nearby town of Caldwell every Sunday to buy beer because Nampa was dry on Sundays. When I was working on my driver's license, I happily went along to get some miles behind the wheel.
- There were only two television stations available on our black and white set. One was the NBC affiliate because we got the Saturday baseball game of the week.
- Dad was a volunteer usher at the Snake River Stampede every summer. This was a huge rodeo that brought all the top cowboys from the entire country to Nampa. Dad wore his boots, cowboy hat and vest while working in the stands. I actually looked up information on the top bull riders just to know something about the sport.
- Minor league baseball was thriving in the form of the class single-A Boise Braves of the Pioneer League. As kids, we used to get free or really cheap (maybe 50 cents) admission tickets and we went to a few games every summer.

BACK TO SANTA MONICA (1962-68)

In the summer of 1962, while my mother, Ronnie and I worked the alfalfa fields spraying weeds, we talked about a vacation back to Santa Monica.

It was agreed that if we all donated about half our earnings, maybe $200, we could go back to California for a week. It would be our first family vacation since the initial trip to Idaho three summers earlier.

My father and I shared the driving on the two-day trip – talk about a change in status for me. I was promoted to the front seat instead of the back. I had a serious role in the trip rather than just killing time in the backseat. For reasons I never learned, my mother chose not to drive.

While back in Santa Monica, we kids were enjoying the beach, reuniting with friends, and relatives. My dad visited his former boss, who offered him his old job back, but at a better wage, reportedly $10,000 annually. He never got that much money, and what did that number mean to us kids, anyway? Later on, in my second year at the Daily Breeze, when I earned $10,000, it was a milestone for me.

The California lifestyle, reunions with family and friends, and the offer of "big bucks" was enough for the Cox Family. We drove back to Idaho, packed up our stuff, and turned around and headed back to California, in time for the school year to start.

Those were exciting times, except for one little detail, my folks learned that my Idaho Driver's License, granted at age 14, would not be honored in California. Or at least that's what they told me. Santa Monica had the big blue busses, and they only cost 15 cents, or maybe a quarter? I soon found myself riding the bus to school.

And there were girls – I remember my friend Pat Williams and I double-dating with Susie Ashton and Myrna Crowell as summer turned to 10th grade. That meant parents driving us to a movie theater, or the beach, or more likely taking the bus. But it was still a date. Fifty years later – imagine this – I have reconnected with Susie and Myrna as Facebook friends.

What an amazing world we live in. Another friend from the early Santa Monica days, Doug Moody, is also on Facebook. These are people who were very important to me in the 1950s and early 1960s.

I returned to Santa Monica in time for the start of school shortly after Labor Day.

Santa Monica High, known far and wide as Samohi, was a great place to be in those days. That was a great time to be a young American. Eisenhower had steered us through the 1950s, playing golf and avoiding controversy. Kennedy was elected in 1960, and we were going to the moon.

Things weren't always so idyllic, of course. The Bay of Pigs Invasion and the Cuban Missile Crisis rocked our civil conscience pretty good. Later we would learn about the troop build-up in Southeast Asia as we rallied to stop Communism's Domino Effect in Vietnam. (Historical note: How well did that work out?)

And in 1963, the assassinations started with the death of JFK in Dallas on Nov. 22. Los Angeles newspapers printed multiple editions all day and I was reading all of them. I was a newspaper junky before I knew newspapers would be my first career.

High school football was the C team – football for younger and smaller guys using a method of combining points for age, height and weight and giving you a number. The smaller the number the more likely you could play on the B or C teams, which were for players not good enough or big enough for Varsity or JV. That was great. I loved playing on the smaller-kid teams. I was probably about 125 pounds in those days anyway.

I was on a C basketball team with two guys who also went on to considerable journalism success, Bruce Jenkins (S.F. Chronicle) and Lyle Spencer (lots of papers, including the New York Post, L.A. Herald-Examiner and The National).

I never made it out of the lower level teams – perhaps it was size, and perhaps it was ability. Although I did have a shot in basketball.

In those days, coaches were not allowed to work with their teams in summer leagues, so the coach would pick somebody "responsible" and hand him the bag of balls and jerseys to serve as player-coach That was the summer after my junior year. I was pretty adept at ball handling and passing the ball – sort of a point guard before that term existed. My summer league team played one night a week at Palisades High, and we were pretty much winning everything. I deluded myself into thinking that if we continued to do well, I might get asked to the varsity as a backup.

Near the end of the summer, we forgot to bring our A game to a contest against Taft High from the Valley. My shooters weren't hitting shots, and I was dribbling down the court near the end of the game, when this little guy with glasses – imagine me calling someone little, and I have worn glasses most of my life – stole the ball from me. Nobody stole the ball from me in those days. I could dribble and handle the ball.

But he stole it, and he was landing on the floor after his layup pretty much sealed the loss for us. I went up in an obvious fake attempt to block the already completed shot, and somehow hit the kid in the head with my knees and tumbled to the floor. Today they'd call that a flagrant foul with ejection automatic.

I just knew that when I came up against the back wall, his entire team converged on me, ready to fight. My two forwards were big African Americans who knew how to fight, and the three of us got our backs to the gymnasium wall and started throwing punches at anybody who came forward. The coach and referee who thought summer basketball was easy money had to break up a brawl. Suffice it to say there were good guys and bad guys in this brawl. And for one of the first times in my life, I was on the wrong side of that equation.

When I called the coach the next day – probably mid-day before I got up my nerve to try and explain what happened – he had already heard. And had made his decision. "There's no room on the varsity for a hot head," said Coach Dick Beede. I wasn't good enough to get away with the behavior I'd displayed. You're not showing leadership when you lose your temper. It took me a few days to realize, but that was the end of my basketball career.

Not that there was much of an upside. I was probably 5-10, fairly athletic, and good with ball skills. But I was not great at anything. I might have made the varsity team as the 11th or 12th man – or maybe I was destined to be that 12th grade Junior Varsity player. Was I ever going to be asked to try out in junior college? Probably not, but I could dream. Until the night I lost it on the court, started a brawl, and got suspended from summer league.

I know there was a lifelong lesson in that outburst.

A year or two earlier, basketball taught me an even costlier lesson.

I was a sophomore – just back from exotic Idaho – and I had a girlfriend. Her name was Stanette, because her father had hoped for a boy named Stan. Anyway, she and I were 14, maybe 15, and moving fast in the exploration stage. Ours was that moment everyone treasures and remembers: Their First Time.

Stanette lived with her two spinster aunts and we were into our lessons about anatomy in a fast and furious way, considering we were 14 years old.

One night after a movie, we stopped in the apartment laundry room for a couple of more lessons, before ending the evening. In those days, girls wore short skirts all the time, with dreadful pantyhose underneath. It was an engineering marvel that on the floor of the apartment house laundry room – cold hard cement – on a Saturday night, I managed to remove all impediments to our climactic moment and we had a couple of minutes of first-ever coital bliss. Did it last two minutes? Probably not. Did we use protection? Of course not. Were we lucky on all counts? Yes.

But the lesson was to come a week later. Stanette wanted to spend more time together. Of course there was a reward. Even if it had to be redeemed on the laundry room floor. But she wanted me to spend Saturday afternoon with her, and I wanted to play basketball with my friends in our regular game at the Lincoln Jr. High gym, where pickup games went on all day. Who would choose basketball over an afternoon of making out and possibly another sexual conquest? A 14-year-old high school sophomore who was a little short on worldly learning. Maybe I thought that since I was "doing it" with Stanette, I'd have the same luck with other girls.

She broke up with me over my desire to spend the afternoon playing basketball and easily found another boyfriend. She was cute and very romantic. It took almost a year before I would get another shot at the level of intimacy I spurned for an afternoon of pickup basketball.

So maybe there are two reasons why I did not become a big basketball star as a teenager, or even much of a fan of the sport as an adult.

RONALD DEAN COX (1949-1989)

My brother Ronnie was born a year and five days after me, on Jan. 4, 1949, also at Santa Monica Hospital. Known as Bobby and Ronnie, we were close for the first 12 or 13 years of our lives, then grew rapidly apart and rarely saw each other as adults.

Part of that was because he spent most of those years behind bars, owing largely to his addiction to heroin. He died in the late 1980s of an overdose while living in a halfway house for recently released prisoners with addiction problems.

My memories of Ronnie are random.

For most of our lives, my parents were determined to treat us equally, ignoring the difference in our ages. If I got a toy, Ronnie got the toy. I got a Daisy BB gun. Ronnie got the same gun. Pictures of us from the 1950s often show us dressed in the same clothes. You'd have thought they wanted twins.

I have a few lasting memories – hang-ups if you will – about this treating two kids equally. Ronnie's path through the judicial system, his addictions, his serious problems in school, may have been more egregious and powerful.

This memory has been embedded for, oh, 50 or 60 years. Talk about lasting.

I was told I could not ride my bike to school until I was in the 4th grade. OK, if that's the standard, I get it. Perhaps we are better bike riders at age 9 than we are at age 8. Surely our judgement is better. Either way, I knew that I would be riding my bike the 8 blocks to McKinley Elementary School in 4th grade.

Then they let Ronnie have the same privilege at the same time – or when he was 8, and in 3rd grade. I was very bitter about that. Bitter enough to carry it around for half a century. How screwed up is that?

I remember he and I playing on the same Little League baseball teams for most of our time in that sport. I was a catcher of some repute and he was a pitcher. But not a star. I don't remember much about other sports in conjunction with Ronnie.

I remember these things:

- When we had returned from Idaho, and I was in 10th grade at Samohi, and he was in 9th grade at Lincoln Junior High, he was suspended from school for bringing a hunting knife to school. It was my knife from Idaho. And it was confiscated. I think there were extenuating circumstances on his behalf. He reportedly was defending a Special Ed kid from a bully, but he didn't know how to do that right.
- There were a couple of times when he wanted to resolve our problems with his fists. He was better at fighting than I was. I figured out that I liked girls and sports a lot more than I did fighting. By about age 14, he was the better fighter.
- He started having troubles in high school, perhaps because I was succeeding. Or maybe there was more to his troubles. I don't remember. Anyway, his school records probably end about the time he was 16. About the same time, he started learning about the County detention system.
- My dad and I made more than a few trips to Wayside Honor Rancho in Saugus, which was L.A. County's main facility for juveniles, and later adults. He was a frequent flyer for mostly minor things.
- By the time he was 18, he'd graduated to adult lockups and started doing drugs seriously. Which meant stealing things to pay for drugs.

- There was a story on the front page of the *Evening Outlook*, Santa Monica's paper, with picture, on the day police arrested the "Pony-Tailed Bandit," after a series of more than a dozen drive-through armed robberies of Photo-Mat stores. Remember them? Remember cameras and film? You'd drive up to this little yellow booth in a parking lot and leave your film, then come back to pick up your pictures a few days later. Ronnie would drive up with a mask on his face and a weapon in hand and rob the Photo-Mat clerk. He later swore that the gun was not real, but the judge didn't believe him. He did hard time in a series of federal prisons. We communicated by mail, and he was constantly asking me to send money to his prison account so he could buy cigarettes and other items.

- When he got out, there was a question about him coming to live with me, but that was a no chance, and he returned to live with some woman he knew in Malibu.

- He'd made front page of the newspaper for a second time a few years later, when my parents were still alive, so perhaps the early 1970s. That was when he went into a Big 5 Sporting Goods store in Santa Monica, bought a rifle, then sat on the curb and put the gun in his mouth and pulled the trigger. But it was not a successful suicide attempt. He shot himself in the part of the brain that is removed for lobotomies. He spent a lot of time in the county hospital and rehab system, and was eventually released.

- I went to see him in Harbor General County Hospital one day. Got to the floor where he was, and outside the room, and saw a guy I didn't recognize, all wired up and bandaged up, and looking very old and very seriously impaired. I could not bring myself to go in and talk to him. That was a story I told no one back then. We had nothing in common before his suicide attempt, and the bullet did not change things.

- Should I have reached out to him then, and at other times? Surely if I were into second guessing, those would be questions I'd ask. But I was never one for regrets, so I just moved on with my life.

- When he died at about the age of 40 – that would be 1989, I believe – I learned about it from a detective who had been called to the halfway house where he was living and found the body. Cause of Death was a heroin overdose. After being clean for months, he'd acquired some very good heroin, and it was apparently too potent for his system. He died alone in that halfway house room.

- He was married at 18 and fathered a daughter named Cherie. She and I and his ex-wife, Christine, talked a few times after the death. They had a small memorial service. I did not attend, but sent money to pay for his cremation.

- Ronnie's wedding was probably the closest he and I ever were after years of going in opposite directions. Pictures show me in a white tuxedo, same as Ronnie, as his best man. I remember also paying for a night in a hotel in the Valley to give them some semblance of a honeymoon. I was departing the next day for the Navy, and boot camp.

I'm sorry there aren't many insights into Ronnie's life, or my parents' attempts to help him out when his troubles started in school and with the law.

I'm not sure my parents understood his problems, or how to deal with them, and I was too busy working out my own issues and moving to a hopefully better life.

ODD JOBS AND A WORK ETHIC (1962-65)

Our first year back in Santa Monica, my first year of high school at Samohi (1962-63) was mostly carefree from my point of view. There was school, sports, girls, and a few odds and ends, like the Cuban Missile Crisis and the beginnings of Vietnam.

Mostly I was focused on the first three (school, sports and girls).

But the work ethic that had been nurtured in Idaho quickly got restarted in Santa Monica. In my junior year at Samohi, I was learning that I probably would not go on to stardom in sports. Not sure exactly when that lesson was driven home, but it was in the works for a long time.

And at the end of 1963, I turned 16, which allowed me to legally work. Not that I hadn't worked for our first year back. During holidays and sometimes summer, there was always a chance to work a few hours doing menial work at Coast Furniture Store, where my dad was manager. I was available to dust furniture, change price tags during sales or inventory, and occasionally help out on the delivery truck.

Those were jobs under the shadow of my father. And realizing that when I turned 16 and could legally drive again, I would need a car, and that my folks would not be providing it. I knew work was important.

Connections through older friends often helped create job opportunities. Jim Siroty worked at Culver City (now Brotman) Memorial Hospital as an orderly, and he heard they needed kitchen help. I applied and was hired for weekends and holidays. Those were 8-hour days every Saturday and Sunday and the odd holidays. It was mostly dishwashing, cleanup, occasionally doing a little light grill cooking or food preparation. But it was a job and that put money in my pocket and I started saving for a car.

Later, when I did get that license, I had my first run-in with the California Traffic system. I got the license on my birthday, Dec. 30, and on Dec. 31, Siroty and I were cruising Hollywood Boulevard for New Year's Eve. Distracted by the many women on the streets, I ran a red light in front of a cop. The juvenile traffic judge suspended my license for a couple of weeks. One day with a license and it was suspended. That's got to be a record.

I had one more harrowing experience with my driver's license later that year. Four of us were driving around Santa Monica in an old clunker I had bought for about $200. Someone mentioned seltzer bottles, so we bought a couple, and two guys used them to spray pedestrians on the sidewalk. Great fun, or so it seemed at the time.

We sprayed one old guy in a suit near the bowling alley at 26th Street, and with the wisdom of youth, drove around the block to come back and look at our merry work. The old guy had gotten into his late model sedan by then and was waiting for us, and started chasing us. Not sure how high-speed the chase was, but it was certainly above the speed limit and was frightening. At one point, he was pulling up next to us and holding out something black in his right hand. I thought it was a gun, and pulled over. All four of us dove to the floor mats.

When we came up, the suburban Santa Monica street was lit up like Christmas. Seems the old guy was a County Marshall, and he was being chased by several of Santa Monica's finest because he was speeding. And it wasn't a gun he was holding out, but his badge.

We were all juveniles, so we were hauled down to the Police Station to be picked up by our parents. All three of the others were scolded, and maybe grounded for a few days.

Since it was well into the evening, by the time my dad arrived to pick me up, he was pretty lit as well. He slammed the seltzer bottle on the linoleum floor, shattering it. By the time the paperwork was processed, I had also received a citation for reckless driving. This led to another license suspension. And another lesson: The driver pays heavily for pranks like that.

Once I got my license back again, I wanted more work, so I applied for and got a job delivering the *Los Angeles Times* on a car route in the early morning hours. I delivered about 350 copies of the paper 7 days a week in West Los Angeles, tossing the paper from the window of my father's car, and then later from a junker that I bought for about $150. On Credit.

Those were some long weekend days, starting with the Times job at 3 a.m. on Saturday, which lasted until about 5:30 or 6 a.m. Sometimes I was able to take a 1-hour nap. Then I went to the hospital and worked 8 hours. Usually Saturday night was some high school or junior college sports event. Then I was back at the Times job Sunday morning for the Big Day, when the paper weighed several pounds and often required two loads to deliver from my dad's station wagon. Sundays took longer because of the size of the paper, so there was no nap before the hospital kitchen job.

Sounds awful all these years later, but I was loving the independence these jobs gave me. Not sure how much money I was making, but maybe $80 a week. Big money for a teenager.

I was learning to get by on limited sleep. And something had to give. It was my grades. After doing pretty well my sophomore year, I got caught up in the work spiral my junior year, and started learning how little effort it took to get a passing grade. My standards were slipping, but my motivation was money, not grades. And nobody at home said much because I was still getting C's. There was one D in trigonometry, and that meant a dreaded summer school class to somehow nudge out a C. But I was OK with being an average student at that point in life.

In my second year at Samohi, I was enrolled in a journalism elective, and met Andy Dimas, who taught journalism and English. Years later, he became a lifelong friend, although we had a rough moment at the end of my junior year.

I wound up in journalism because English had been pretty easy for me, and some counselor was looking for an elective to fit my schedule. Turns out that counselor – who I do not remember – did me one of life's biggest favors and put me in position for a lifelong career.

In journalism class, you learn the basics of reporting (who, what, when, where, why and how) and something called the Inverted Pyramid.

Nothing terribly complicated. You start with the most important aspect of the story and continue writing until the least important, at the bottom of the inverted pyramid. That way, if you have written too much for the space editors have allotted to your story, they can easily cut (or edit) from the bottom and excise only the lesser facts.

The basics of journalism proved to be a foundation that helped me in everything I did in life, including education after I retired from journalism. Sorting and prioritizing facts from top to bottom, and writing them in a clean and concise manner. If you can do that, I would suggest you can handle most of life's challenges.

Journalism was a quick fit for me. And I was surprisingly good enough at it to get a lot of assignments and move into consideration for a leadership position the next year.

My thinking was that I should be named Sports Editor of The SAMOHI (the paper's name as well as the school's nickname) for my senior year, but when it was announced at the end-of-year Journalism banquet, I was runner-up. First loser. My friend Doug Moody, whose dad happened to be our printer at Santa Monica City College, was chosen for the position. I know now, decades later, that Dimas made the right decision for the paper and the relationship with the man we could not do without. Couldn't see that then, though.

Years later, after another mutual friend from Samohi, Mike Pardridge, made contact and I helped him get a couple of jobs at LAUSD, we were part of a campaign to get Dimas recognition for his Distinguished Contributions to Samohi. We reunited at the awards banquet at Riviera Country Club with fellow Samohi grads and working journalists.

In his memoirs, Dimas used a comment from me about covering a Super Bowl and looking around to see Bruce Jenkins (San Francisco *Chronicle*), Lyle Spencer (Denver *Rocky Mountain News*) Mike Martínez (*New York Times*) and myself.... and wondering if any other high school journalism instructor ever had four graduates in the same press box covering a major event like the Super Bowl.

Later when I read Andy Dimas' memoirs – he's 10 years my elder – I learned how important that was to him as a young teacher. Mr. Dimas and I connected a number of times in recent years, including when he had cancer … we both battled that demon. He lives in Santa Rosa and we stay in touch.

Pardridge and wife Janice Hickey (later a colleague in education when she was assistant superintendent at El Segundo school district) and I shared a few moments and became close … until they dropped off the face of the map after deciding to leave education.

I have nothing but good will for Samohi journalism graduates, even the guy who was sports editor in my stead. Interestingly, he never held a job in newspaper or sports journalism.

We did not know it at the time, but Dimas was deep in the closet when he was teaching us, yet later had several very long-term relationships with his partners. As we grew and matured, it did not seem like a big thing.

Journalism class at Samohi was the beginning of a lifelong pursuit for me and was followed shortly by the biggest decision of my young life. Hanging out with my older friends Jim Siroty and Joe Marek, I was learning how newspaper sports sections covered high school sports. Mostly with a network of volunteers and lowly paid interns who manned the phones on Friday nights as correspondents called in the results.

Each paper had its own network and there was sharing of resources. The Hollywood *Citizen-News* was known for its prep coverage in those days, mostly because of an ambitious high school teacher named Jerry Weiner, who doubled as the prep sports editor at the *Citizen-News*.

Something unfortunate happened during that fall, and the paper fired Weiner. Rumors were that when a movie was filming in the newspaper offices, a secretary left her portable typewriter overnight, and Weiner was accused of stealing it. He was fired and the paper was scrambling to get help. Marek knew somebody, who hired him and his two buddies (Siroty and me) to start that Friday night. We were frantically taking calls, writing short stories on games we had not attended, and loving every minute of it.

I had a couple of weekends where I went from the *Citizen-News* on Friday night, to the *Times* car route on early Saturday morning, to the hospital all day Saturday. I can't recall how or when I found a little sleep. But I knew I could not keep this up.

The decision: The *Citizen-News* job was more exciting, might lead to a future, and was in journalism, which I was madly in love with. But it would not pay as much as the combined hospital cafeteria job and *Times* delivery route.

I'm sure I asked my dad, and I'm betting he weighed in on behalf of more money – since there was never a spare nickel in the family coffers. But I was already becoming independent, and after a few weekends of three jobs and no sleep, I made the call.

I was going to work as a part-time sports writer for the *Citizen-News* at $1.50 or $2 an hour – with no guarantee of hours – and gave up the other two jobs.

My grades didn't improve, because I was loving the *Citizen-News* so much, I worked every night. Nobody told me not to come in, so I was there 5 or 6 nights a week. Not fulltime, But I got my hours up to 28 or 30 or 32 – and I was getting paid for something I truly loved.

Sometime that spring, Marek and Siroty pulled a prank that got them fired, calling in a phony basketball score on a night when one of the lesser lights of the sports staff was in charge. I took the call and mentioned to this guy named Mannie that the names seemed odd (Jack Mihoff, for example) but he said, "Those East L.A. kids have funny names. Write a paragraph and slap a headline on it."

I survived that, and my love for the excitement of sports journalism meant I was staying on all school year. By the summer, when high school sports took a hiatus, I was worried I would not have a job. But the sports editor convinced the managing editor to put me on as a vacation substitute filling in as everything from copy editor to copy boy.

After that summer, I was hooked. I loved working on the news desk with the salty old dogs of the newsroom. These were veterans of a life in journalism, knew a lot of life's truths, and were willing to share with a bright-eyed and eager young apprentice.

And when school started the next fall – my senior year – I was entrenched in the job I gave up more money for. And my work habits had marked me in the eyes of management. I was offered a chance to work a Saturday morning news desk shift, after working Friday nights on high school sports. I was grabbing a couple of hours sleep on the editor's couch from 1 to 3 a.m., then working on the serious side of life on the news desk. I learned a lot about news judgement and how to make decisions in those days.

Oh, and I was still a high school student. My senior year was a bit of a blur. Working five nights a week on high school sports at the *Citizen-News,* plus Saturday mornings on the news desk. Can't remember ever carrying a book home from school in those days.

My grades were tolerable, although I was no longer an A-B student. I might have gotten A's in journalism, but probably more like low B's and mostly C's on everything else. Years later, I found an old transcript and realized I was almost exactly in the middle of the graduating class, something like No. 500 of 1,000 graduates. Nothing memorable as a student. But I had gotten a great start on a lifelong career.

A memory from my senior year stands out because of how different life was in 1965.

I was taking an English elective called Biography, from a teacher who was the living model for the Beach Boys song, "She's Abigail Beecher, my history teacher." If you don't remember the song, Abigail Beecher was a hot blonde who drove a souped-up muscle car and was only a few years older than the kids she taught.

My teacher was Patricia Noblin – amazing the names you remember, right? – a hot blonde, who drove a Dodge Charger, and who seemed to understand things. In those days, before a final exam, you would spend an hour in the classroom, presumably studying. Well, I was barely keeping my eyes open, likely from a late night on the sports desk, and she called me outside the classroom. Noblin suggested I go across the street and get a cup of coffee and smoke a couple of cigarettes.

Does that sound outrageous? We had an open campus. We all smoked – this was 1965 – and she trusted this 17-year-old kid to go get himself tuned up for the test. I returned on time and did pretty well on the test. Always remembered Noblin. She was my second most favorite high school teacher behind Andy Dimas, who watered the journalism seed that sent me off on a lifelong journey.

MY CAREER AS A GREAT
PLAYER (1962-LATER)

The older I get, the better I used to be in sports.

When son Randy made his first varsity football appearance as a junior at Torrance High, he had already topped me. I peaked out on the C team at Santa Monica High after two years as a sophomore and junior. When daughter Allie made varsity in both softball and volleyball as a sophomore at West High, she was way ahead of me. And when she played four years in college, she buried any comparisons I might have made.

In truth, I have tried to talk a good sports legacy for all these years, but I was too small, too slow and too ordinary in all of the main sports. But I tried hard.

I was the classic utility infielder/backup catcher, if you will. I worked harder, learned the rules, showed up early, practiced more, and did all the things those of us not gifted with great skills had to do. I had a few moments. I was a pretty good catcher in Little League, and continued into Pony or Colt League when we returned to Santa Monica, but I was clearly out of my league. I never even entertained playing baseball in high school because those teams were really good. A guy named Rick Monday preceded me by a year at Samohi, and he was the first draft pick in the first-ever baseball draft. He hung around the majors for 15 or 20 years, and remains a broadcaster for the Dodgers.

I did manage to play two years of football and basketball, albeit on the C teams. In those days, high school sports had an age/size scorecard and if you were a combination of young and light, you could play on the C or B teams before moving up to JV or Varsity. We had four teams in both sports. Later they changed to the current structure of Frosh/Soph, JV and Varsity, although Frosh/Soph is getting phased out in many sports at a lot of schools.

Let's talk about my heroics.

Well ....

In football, on the Samohi C team I was a 2-way player (many of the 20 or so players were). I played wingback on offense and outside linebacker on defense. I was also the kicker for kickoffs (we attempted one kicked PAT and no field goals in two years), and the backup punter and backup quarterback.

My career as the backup quarterback consisted on one play in a game we were winning easily at Redondo. Coach Bob Harris, a young teacher who had played as a backup lineman at UCLA and was destined to become a very successful varsity coach at Blair High in Pasadena, felt the same about throwing the football as most in his generation. Three things can happen when you pass and two are bad. In short, we ran about 95 percent of the time, and never threw the ball down the field. Except in practice. We threw a lot of practice passes then, and felt good about it. Just not good enough to pass in games.

Of course, we were fundamentally sound enough that we didn't have to. We were winning games easily the old-fashioned way by running the ball between the tackles, and playing solid defense.

But in this rout at Redondo, Coach Harris put me in at quarterback. So, I called a pass play. Imagine the backup getting to call plays. Well, we didn't practice pass blocking much, and I'd called for a long pass, and the defenders were in my face before I got off a feeble deflected pass that fell untouched halfway between me and the receiver. Next play, the regular was back at quarterback, handing off to the running backs. That was my entire career as a high school quarterback.

I was probably a little better at basketball, because that was a game where you could work hard and often without anybody's help. Although I was probably 5-foot-9 in my sneakers, I was our center on the C team,

31

although my skills were better attuned to playing what is now called point guard.

There were later slow-pitch softball teams – continuing into my 50s – which was a great chance to hang out with friends like Jim Benz, Mike Sremba, Nick Duvalley and John Catozzi. We all brought different skills to the table but mostly it was about being on a co-ed team and having fun.

While those were the mainstay guys of the co-ed team, we rotated through a lot of female players. On occasion, we'd even get a very good female player. One year we found a 20-something girl who had played outfield at CSUN, on a Division III team, and she was a major asset. Never mind that she was with us mostly to find a boyfriend – and wasn't interested in our mature crew of players so she moved on before long.

In many ways, my favorite sports outings were as part of a baseball team of sports writers. I was usually the catcher, and we got to play at Anaheim and Dodger stadiums on Saturday mornings, usually against a team of young employees like clubhouse guys, assistant trainers, scouts, front office guys.

I also used to play in a few of the Dodgers Hollywood Stars games when a team of writers and sportscasters played the shills for the real stars. I had one of my worst days in sports in one of these games and one of my best.

The worst: I was playing shortstop. I was also coaching a little league baseball team in those days, so I arranged for my team to come and see the game. Fortunately, they were out in the right-field pavilion when I committed three errors in one inning. Booted two ground balls and threw one away. And there were 40,000 people in the stands. I tried to build on my mistakes in practice with my team, but most were more interested in the Dodger Dogs than they were in my play.

'The best moment came when an actor from M*A*S*H named Jamie Farr (he played Corporal Klinger), came to the plate. His bit was that he was going to be a Swish Hitter. You had to have watched the show to get the reference. On his first pitch, he hit a pop foul to the right side, near the visiting team dugout. The real players (Atlanta Braves in those days) were in the dugout to watch. And I came charging over to try to catch the popup at the dugout rail, with Klinger yelling behind me, "Drop it, drop it." He wanted to Swish (switch) to lefthanded batting. But I had a chance to make a real catch, and a couple of the real Braves were standing at the rail, keeping me from falling into the dugout. As if I were a real player. The heck with Klinger's bit – I made the catch.

There was also a moment in a Hollywood Stars game at Anaheim when an actor named Joe Santos from the Rockford Files and later NCIS was trying to score from second on a ball to the outfield, and one of our players made a great throw to the plate. I had the ball and this guy slammed into me in the type of collision that used to happen a lot in baseball. We went ass over teakettle but I held onto the ball and he was out. A sequence of three pictures made the front page of the Anaheim *Bulletin* newspaper the next day. I'm sure it was because he was a favorite TV actor, but I'd like to think my blocking the plate and holding on to the ball was a factor.

But probably my most success in sports came later when I got into skiing after my parents died and Lorraine and I split up in late 1974. Skiing was addictive and I quickly learned there was an even greater high in ski racing.

The ski clubs organized leagues and had competitions four times a year at Mammoth Mountain. You were grouped by ability, based on a handicap formula, and you raced against a dozen or 15 similarly rated athletes.

I threw myself into this and quickly because one of the top regulars. I was a pace-setter for all or our L.A. based leagues, meaning I was one of a handful of consistent racers who would run the course before the others to establish a handicap.

We would later race on a more demanding course. I could regularly place in the top handful, and occasionally snagged a win. Ski racing produced a lot of trophies and plagues, so I'd have to say this was the highlight of my sports career.

THE BRIDGE YEARS (1964-67)

Once I realized that my life was not going to be spent on a sporting field, the next best thing was writing about sports.

That started in high school, when I wound up in the Journalism class taught by Andy Dimas, and which led me to some great contacts, some fortuitous opportunities, and all the games a guy could ever want.

Although there is considerable overlap along the way, here's a rough sketch of my newspaper sports career:

In November 1963, I was hired as a part-timer at the Hollywood *Citizen-News* to answer calls from high school coaches and stringers, take information for and type up the box scores, and write a paragraph or two about the game. Note that I was a month shy of my 17th birthday. I got this job like many others in my early life, through good luck and great contacts.

After working every Friday night and many others through my junior year in high school, my love affair with sports journalism was in full bloom. That summer, I was retained to work as a copy boy, and got a chance to learn aspects of the newsroom and the newspaper world that I never would have learned anywhere else.

By the summer of 1965, after graduating from high school, I became a full-time high school sports writer. I was coordinating the coverage of several other part time writers, and writing two game stories a day on football Fridays (one afternoon game, one night game), and often a Saturday night game. These were on-deadline, get-the-facts straight and get-it-done kind of stories. Football turned to basketball, then spring was track and field and baseball.

Luckily for me, I sort of understood track and field although I was never fast, strong, nor agile enough to compete. My coverage of high school track led me to get to know Maxwell Stiles, the venerable sports columnist and long-time track buff of the *Citizen-News*. I wound up accompanying him to major track meets – they would draw 40,000 at the Coliseum in those days – and he would mentor me on the business. A couple of years later, when Max retired, he mentioned me in his speech at the Century Plaza hotel before 700 sports luminaries as one of the best up-and-coming young writers he'd ever met. I was 19 at the time.

My relationship with Max, who was probably 70 at the time, was the first of many mentorships that worked for me in life. Later, Jack Hawn, the sports editor who left for a couple of years to write TV scripts and later returned, also helped me in many ways.

In those years between high school and the Navy, the *Citizen-News* was my life. But there were a couple of other jobs that helped me understand the world.

There was a social group called a travel club, which owned or leased an older plane, and flew off to cool destinations. They were headed to the Indianapolis 500 in 1966, and I was invited. I made some great contacts on that trip, and wound up working and/or volunteering my time with the club for the rest of the year.

The had an office at Burbank Airport, and I would start my days there, working the counter and helping sell the club concept to interested travelers. It was never a huge success, but it was a lot of fun.

Through that connection, I met an airport jack of all trades named Lou Torrey, who had some jobs at the West Imperial Terminal at LAX. He would head up a crew that handled charter flights, which included everything from groups of Irishmen and women returning to the old country for a visit, to the growing wave of planes taking servicemen to Vietnam.

I worked the counter, checked in passengers, weighed luggage, then helped load luggage into the baggage hold of the plane. This was all before the current computerized systems, so this was pure labor.

Lou was sort of the sub-contractor who worked for the charter airlines, and he brought his own crew to handle the work. It was very casual and we were paid in cash. Imagine just showing up to work at an airport today.

I drove baggage trucks and even the truck called the Honey Bucket, which was hooked up to the airplane restrooms. I was willing to take on any task.

One night they needed somebody to drive the fuel truck – a giant semi that I had no experience driving – yet because I was young, bullet-proof and stupid, I agreed to drive it out to the plane. I remember struggling with the multiple gears, but somehow got this giant inflammable disaster across a couple runways to the airplane. When somebody else started fueling the plane, I realized what a crazy idea it was for me to drive something that dangerous on the active taxiways of one of the world's busiest airports. At night.

I told the boss I couldn't drive it back to the charter terminal, and one of the more experienced guys – one who probably had a license for a truck and trailer – brought it back. And I realized I was way too close to a potential major disaster.

But when you are young and don't realize how dumb you are, things like that happened. At least they did in my life.

The years between high school and the Navy were exciting ones for me, and when I left for my Naval service in January of 1968, it was knowing that I had started to make my mark in newspapers and had a career to come back to in Southern California.

COLLEGE LIFE AND PRE-NAVY DAYS (1965-68)

Graduation from Samohi was not a major moment in my life. I don't remember what I did that night, but attending Disneyland's Grad Night was definitely not on the agenda. I had pretty much separated myself from high school friends by then, and was focusing on those I knew from work.

Among the things on my agenda in summer of 1965: Working my part-time job at the *Citizen-News*, registering for college at Santa Monica City College, avoiding the draft, and getting an apartment.

I was on top of the job situation, and found a way to get nearly full-time hours at my part-time gig. I was going to college, not because I wanted to, but because that was the era of the Vietnam War, and the ramp-up to us having a force of half a million soldiers, sailors and others in a country most of us couldn't find on the map.

The Selective Service Act required every male to register on or about his 18th birthday. Imagine if we ever have a draft again – will it be male only? I don't think so. And shortly after registration, you were given a card designating your status. If you were I-A, you were prime for processing into the Army with a likely ticket to Southeast Asia.

How did you avoid being I-A? Assuming you passed the physical, you had three choices: 1. Go to college, 2. Get married and have kids, or 3. Go to Canada. Since the latter two did not seem likely for me, I registered at SMCC. In those days, the community colleges were known as City Colleges, or Junior Colleges. Like now, they were designed to cover your first two years, with most of the basic classes. And they were free. We may have paid $20 or some insignificant amount for an ID card. You did have to buy books – that was a shock for most of us – but that was the golden era of education in California and college was pretty much free.

While many of my friends had been fast-tracked to major colleges by parents with influence, affluence, or a history of college education in their families, I was pretty much forging my own path. My parents provided a roof over my head, and love and encouragement, but they came from families where high school education was optional and college was not on the agenda.

I remember two discussions about college during my time at Samohi.

- I was in one of those half-semester guidance courses popular in those days. You were supposed to tell the class the college you were looking at. Since I wasn't, when called upon, I looked at the shelf of catalogues in front of me, and picked the name that was easiest to read. Smith College. Having proudly made that choice, the teacher congratulated me on wanting to be a pioneer, and the first male ever to attend Smith College. I'm pretty sure the red on my face was visible to one and all.

- Once I got interested in journalism, I learned that the University of Missouri was known as the premier Journalism program in the country. So, I decided I would go there. I was perhaps 15, and very naïve, so I told my parents my dream. Their reaction was pretty much the same as when I'd asked for a new baseball glove, or a radio, or, pretty much anything. "We can't afford that," they said. So SMCC it was.

  Which led me to Santa Monica City College, derisively called High School with Ashtrays. Again, you have to put this in context – almost everyone smoked in those days. That was about the time the Surgeon General determined that smoking caused cancer and people died. But nobody was ready to believe it. Cigarettes were the major advertisers on television, and radio, and dominated billboards all over America.

I was a 2-pack-a-day Marlboro smoker my last year in high school, and by fall of 1965, that was a habit I brought with me to SMCC.

I had also started acquiring a taste for Scotch Whisky. Our neighbor across the court (six small houses on a lot – popular in the 1950s and '60s but virtually extinct now), was taking on the task of teaching me adult habits. Dick Cordell was 3 or 4 years older than me, and attending San Fernando Valley State College (later to become Cal State Northridge). He and I started hanging out. His mother, for her own reasons and in behavior that today might be frowned upon, spent many evenings teaching her son and I how to drink Scotch, how to kiss, and how to treat ladies.

That was the summer of 1965, when we were indeed branching out and learning to live and love, while many of our peers were getting shipped out to Vietnam.

There was also a major social upheaval in Los Angeles called the Watts Riots. The first one. History will later talk about the Riots of 1992 after the Rodney King verdicts. But this was the summer when American cities learned to riot.

While South Central L.A. (Watts) was becoming a war zone, with National Guard troops joining LAPD in trying to quiet the disturbance that spread over many nights, I was getting off a night shift at the *Citizen-News* and stopping at Gazzarri's, a club on the Sunset Strip. I was dressing the part in those days, and somehow, they overlooked my baby-face and let me in most bars and clubs. I never had a fake ID.

While my parents and everyone else were watching the riots on black-and-white TV, I was meeting a 20-something young lady and wound up at her apartment for the night. Big event in my summer of 17. When I returned home the next morning, my mother was in despair, and my dramatic friend, Dick Cordell, was rushing out to me saying, "thank God, you're alive."

Alive, hell, I was wearing a shit-eating grin because I'd spent the night with a 23-year-old woman. Yeah, I was very alive.

Remember the context. No cell phones and I wasn't going to call my parents at 1 or 2 a.m. to let them know I was going home with some older woman. I wasn't worried about the riots.

That may have been the catalyst that led me to the decision a month later to move out of my parents' house. I was 17 and it was September of 1965. My freshman year of college was starting, and I was making maybe $400 a month. Why wouldn't I move out?

It was so much simpler then. You looked at the classified ads in the back of the newspaper, found a vacancy, visited it, and if you didn't scare the manager, you got the place. Since I dressed older, and presumably acted older than my years, I moved into an apartment on Entrada Drive in the Santa Monica Canyon, across from Will Rogers State Beach.

I was paying $130 a month in rent – and the manager let me pay the security deposit in three installments. He was also good enough to pick up an occasional bottle of scotch or six-pack of beer for me at the corner liquor store, since I'd admitted I wasn't 21 yet. I'm pretty sure I admitted to 19. I was a college student and part-time sports writer.

And I was on my way to an exciting stretch. When I started at SMCC, I was meeting women who hadn't looked at me in high school. Maybe it was because I was developing a gift of gab, or maybe because I was sports editor of the weekly school newspaper and my picture ran over a column on the back page, but I was learning to socialize faster than I was learning Political Science, or Spanish.

On several occasions, I'd leave a class in the company of a young lady, and we'd wind up at my beachfront apartment. The 1960s were as good as the stories you may have heard.

One of my bad habits was giving out keys to my apartment to young ladies. I also gave one to Jim Siroty, my friend and sometime co-worker at the *Citizen-News*.

That practice of giving out keys came back to haunt me when I came home one night and both beds were taken – one by Siroty, the other by a girl that had moved on from me romantically but needed a crash pad – and I wound up on the couch.

I started collecting and keeping track of keys after that.

My work at the *Citizen-News* paid for the apartment, my status as a full-time student kept the military at bay, and I was living a good life. I would even take my dirty clothes over to my parents' house and my mother would wash them.

I was not very political, but I knew about Vietnam, and was aware that the best president ever in the eyes of young people had been assassinated in 1963. His brother was running for president when he was slain. So was Martin Luther King Jr. And there were riots in a lot of cities across America.

There were also the slayings of four students at Kent State University by the National Guard after an anti-war protest. It was a tumultuous time in America.

Aside from the civil unrest, I had one harrowing moment late one summer night. I had been volunteering at the offices of a travel club at Burbank Airport during the day, then working nights at the newspaper. I was also visiting with future wife Lorraine Quinn and her family in Glendale.

In short, I was spending a lot of time on the freeways.

One night, around midnight, I fell asleep while driving on the Santa Monica Freeway. My compact little Volkswagen square-back ripped up a large chunk of the chain-link fencing that divided the freeways in those days. When it came to a stop, surprisingly, I was unhurt.

The LAPD officers handling the case – not sure why CHP was not on the accident – were my friends, right up to when the tow truck was hooking up my car. Suddenly they decided to hook me up.

"Mr. Cox, when was the last time you were in Alameda County?"

"Where's Alameda County?"

I wound up in a single cell in the West L.A. Precinct for about two hours on a warrant charging that I had broken out of the Alameda County Jail in the Bay Area. When it was determined that was not me, I was released in the middle of the night. I was never arrested. Just held to make sure I was not the culprit they were looking for.

Unfortunately, I was never able to ask my brother, but my suspicion was he had used my name and birthday while he was involved in some caper in Oakland.

Later, I found out that my car and I had torn up 88 feet of freeway fence when Cal Trans sent me a bill to repair that amount of chain-link. I hope my insurance paid it, although they did not pay off on the car, which was a total loss.

Cal Trans soon started replacing chain-link dividers with the concrete barriers you see now.

In the summer, I was interning at the elbow of Maxwell Stiles, and while ostensibly there to write about the high school athletes, it was also to learn from a master.

Because I was a willing protégé, Max Stiles was happy to open other doors for me. When he went on vacation in August, I was his choice to cover a couple of Rams exhibition games at the Coliseum. I went from covering Santa Monica High and SMCC to the Rams without much of a qualification process.

It was an exciting time for me and I could pretty much have as many hours as I wanted, and the *Citizen-News* was paying me $2 an hour to do it. Later, I found out that minimum wage for union starting reporters was $83 a week (basically the $2 an hour I was getting). Top scale was $164 a week, back in 1965.

I was learning lessons about life, mostly, but also paying attention to what was around me. After registering for the draft on my birthday in 1965, and receiving my II-S draft deferment because of my student status, I became aware that most American men were going to serve. I could hold off the draft for four years, if I could keep up my interest as a student.

But in truth, the best thing about my time at SMCC was my status as sports editor of the weekly paper, *The Corsair*. Although I was not selected for my high school paper, I was an easy choice here, and I loved it. We took a journalism class from a teacher who had been a society editor (another anachronism) on a paper in Nebraska once, but who had minimal qualifications. Next to her classroom was a newsroom, with a copy desk – and ashtrays! – and I met and fell in-like with Maureen Casey.

She was a year ahead of me and was the editor of the paper. She was smart, sassy, well-dressed and everything I wanted in a girlfriend. Except she was untouchable, because she believed an editor should not date a staff member. We spent a lot of time together, became great friends, but never anything more. She made hanging out in *The Corsair* Newsroom my favorite place before, between and after classes.

I was meeting women through the *Citizen-News*, and most were considerably older, although that didn't seem to be a problem. The photo editor taught me that being well dressed usually meant being served alcohol without an ID, especially in upscale places like hotel bars.

One of the photographers, a nerdy little guy with a crewcut, coke-bottle glasses and a bow-tie, had a Playboy Club key. It was a major status thing at the time. He let me borrow it and I took a couple of dates to the famed Playboy Club on Sunset Blvd.

And the rising female star at the Citizen-News, Mari K. Quinn, was showing me the ropes about making up a newspaper (taking the advertising layouts, adding stories, and pictures) and how to make editing decisions.

We were growing close, and went out a few times. At a Dodger game, I made an off-hand reference to going to get us a couple of beers, "If I can" (since I was only 19 years old) Turns out I was served, but that brought up the discussion of my age. While it wasn't a major problem at the time, before long she was introducing me to her younger sister, Lorraine.

And that's another story for a couple of later chapters, since Lorraine Quinn would become my wife and mother of my first daughter.

But first came the Navy.

I was aware that Jim Siroty had been on a year-long waiting list for the Navy Reserve, and had finally gotten his call. The Navy Reserve, like the Air Force Reserve, was a great option to the

Army and almost certain duty in Vietnam. I got on the waiting list before I ever registered for the draft.

Towards the holiday season in 1966, I received a call from the Navy recruiter, who said he had a spot for me, if I was willing to attend basic training (boot camp) starting in January 1967. Since I was not loving school – other than the newspaper and Maureen Casey – and I knew I would have to do something, I enlisted in the Navy Reserve in December 1966.

I was ordered to San Diego for three months of boot camp starting in January 1967. I dropped out of SMCC without finishing my third semester. Probably ruined my mediocre GPA by doing that. But I never looked back. Never inquired about a transcript, or tried to use any of those classes on future educational adventures, either.

Talk about a lifestyle change. From living the life of a free-wheeling young bachelor student/sports writer, to what amounted to incarceration as a recruit. And I was thrown in with a company of other young men that I had little in common with.

There was one young man who I looked up to and who I knew about. Vance Peterson had been a star hurdler at Occidental College (near L.A.) whose exploits I had written about during the summer when I was covering track meets. Decades later, I discovered he had returned to Oxy in an administrative capacity and become president of the school.

In boot camp, he was chosen the recruit chief petty officer, in charge of our 64-man company. I was given a lesser job, educational petty officer, but mostly I was just marking time during this stretch. We were up early, ran or marched everywhere, learned to hand-wash our uniforms, and lived a very spartan life.

When our basic training was over, the Navy didn't know what to do with us, because we were the first group of Reservists to take the full boot camp. We were sent back to our Reserve Units (mine was Santa Monica, across from the airport), with instructions to attend meetings every Tuesday night until the end of the year when we would be called to active duty for two years.

During that stretch from April through December of 1966, I was learning the Navy way. I learned that if you applied for an "A" School, or basic training in a trade, and got it, that guaranteed you would work in that field. I learned about the combined services and their Defense Information School for Journalism, and got some great letters of recommendation from folks at the *Citizen-News, an*d was accepted.

My orders were to report to DINFOS at Fort Benjamin Harrison, Ind., in the second week of January 1968.

This was also a tumultuous time for our country, aside from the Vietnam War. A Navy communications ship (read communications as a synonym for spy) was captured by the North Koreans without a shot being fired and its crew was imprisoned for more than a year. This was the USS Pueblo.

That was one of the topics we discussed at DINFOS.

The school was one of the best things that ever happened to me. Classes all day, five days a week, in journalism, photography, public relations, and learning the military way. We were in a group that included sailors, marines, airmen and soldiers, we were almost all men, save for a couple of women from the army and marines. And it was taught by combined military and civilian instructors.

While I was not a particularly motivated student at SMCC, I found instant motivation at DINFOS. I learned that the top student in each service in each class got his choice of duty assignment. Since I was stuck on a base outside Indianapolis, in the winter, with no money, I got motivated.

As the culmination of our 12 weeks, we were divided up into six staffs, with each staff having an editor selected by the advisors, and asked to produce an 8-page base newspaper in one week. I was chosen an editor, and threw myself into the task. My paper finished second, and 50 years later, looking at the six papers, I still think I was jobbed. Ours was the most professional looking paper.

But that did not detract from my grades. I graduated "With Honors" as the top sailor, and second overall in the class.

After I had worked through my Hemingway phase – thinking I needed to volunteer for Vietnam to cover a war – I had to fill out a dream sheet with my preferences for shore or sea duty assignments. I knew I did not want to live in the U.S. on my salary of $55 every two weeks – even with free room and board – so I put in for overseas duty, with Spain and Japan my two choices. I also picked cruisers over aircraft carriers if I had to go on a ship.

The Navy lived up to its promise and assigned me to the Naval Air Station, Atsugi, Japan.

I was on to more adventures.

NAVY JOURNALIST IN JAPAN (1968-70)

My Biggest Adventure began as The Longest Day at L.A. International Airport on a Thursday in May 1968. I boarded a plane to San Francisco, followed by a bus ride to Travis Air Force Base outside the Bay Area. I had orders and a guaranteed seat on a flight that would stop in Honolulu, then Wake Island, and finally land at Yokota AFB in the outskirts of Tokyo.

Because it was still spring in the U.S., I was traveling in my Navy dress blues. Not bad for L.A. or S.F. weather, but a little warm for Honolulu, and later Wake Island.

The trip took more than 24 hours total, including about 20 hours on the charter flight that started at Travis. I was sitting next to a young Navy wife and her baby for most of the flight. She was joining her husband in Wake Island. I was headed off to what we stereotypically called the Orient. The 100 percent full Braniff Airlines chartered flight was not serving cocktails. This was the Vietnam Era, when the U.S. Military was chartering planes from every U.S. airline and running dozens of full flights a day to the Far East, with many landing in Vietnam.

I had dodged the Vietnam bullet by finishing first among the Navy journalists in my class at DINFOS, and got one of my first choices of duty. I was assigned to the Naval Air Station at Atsugi, Japan.

One of the things the veteran sailors at DINFOS had shared was to call your assigned office when you arrive in a foreign country. After landing at Yokota, I called the Public Affairs Office at Atsugi, and talked to the duty sailor, who said he would be waiting for me when the bus from Yokota arrived. That was probably about midnight, so Journalist 2nd Class Harlan Burr took me to the barracks where he was quartered and got me settled in.

Waiting for the bus, I killed a couple of hours at the enlisted club at Yokota, enjoying my first taste of 25-cent military cocktails. I had managed to take the edge off after 20 hours of flying, then slept on the bus through the Japanese countryside.

Burr gave me a tour of the office and the base on the weekend, and also introduced me to the town called Sagami-Otsuka outside the base. He also told me the PAO office was waiting for my arrival and that of a couple of other sailors. They were ramping up from two enlisted journalists and an officer to a staff that would include the officer, a chief, four enlisted journalists and a photographer. All part of the buildup of U.S. troops in the Far East, which was at its peak in 1968.

After an official check-in on Monday, I found that even though my assignment was the Public Affairs Office, the Navy still had an unfortunate and outdated tradition of "orientation" for new sailors ranked E-3 and below. That wasn't so much to teach you about the base, the Navy or the country. It was a reminder of where you stood on the pecking order. You reported each morning and learned how to handle chores like mopping floors, and cleaning up the yard outside the Captain's quarters. Since I was an E-3 (although designated a Journalist Seaman) I had to put in my days.

But I was free at night to learn about the joys of the Enlisted Men's (EM) Club – the Navy was a little slow in acknowledging that it had a few women in the ranks. I also started learning about the joys of nightly liberty (permission to leave base until 11:30 p.m.).

Finally, after a week on the new guys' detail, I was able to put on a dress uniform and report to work at the PAO office. I joined Lieutenant Junior Grade Bill Jamieson, plus Journalists 2nd Class Harlan Burr and Russ (Stoney) Stone. As well as a secretary and an interpreter. Burr was soon to depart at the end of his tour, and I was officially his replacement.

My first assignment was to take over the two sports pages of the weekly newspaper called *The Skywriter*, in honor of Atsugi's status as the Navy's largest air base in Japan. I would do a couple of other stories each week as well, but my main assignment was the sports section.

Atsugi was home to three squadrons (large commands in their own right): One flew COD (carrier onboard delivery) missions to bring replacement troops, mail, supplies, etc., to aircraft carriers; the helicopter squadron rescued downed pilots, and the third flew surveillance (spy) missions. All were rotated regularly back and forth to Vietnam, a couple of countries to the south.

Atsugi's history dated back to use by the Japanese Air Force in World War II, but from an American perspective, it had an even more significant role: General Douglas MacArthur landed at Atsugi to accept the Japanese surrender at the end of World War II.

The base was large enough that senior officers and enlisted men were allowed to bring wives and families for extended tours. There was housing on base, a movie theater, clubs and restaurants, a bowling alley, and a large sports program.

The military in the 1960s believed in the morale building aspect of sports. We had a civilian athletic director named George Najarian, who would become one of my best friends and mentors during my time in Japan. We fielded varsity teams in football, basketball and softball, as well as a thriving intramural program in all of those sports and a few others, including boxing. We also had a golf course, which hosted major military tournaments and the Japanese pro tour. I had no trouble filling up my sports pages, and got to know a lot of Navy men who participated,

Najarian was a member of the 1950 University of California football team, famed in those days, who had discovered Japan during his three years of Naval service as a lieutenant. He found a way to get a job on base with a lofty GS (Government Service) pay status, on-base housing, and was a scratch golfer.

I learned a lot about making the system work for you from Najarian. He found ways to get me assigned to cover the basketball team when it flew to tournaments in other Japanese areas, as well as one 10-day tournament in Taiwan (Nationalist China). He also made sure I was on the trip when he took the football team to the Philippine Islands – no Navy man should miss a trip to Subic Bay, headquarters of the U.S. Navy in the Far East. I also traveled when we sent a team of boxers to a big competition at Iwakuni Marine Corps base in southern Japan.

Most importantly, during my first year in Japan when I was still working for minimum wage as an E-3, he found a way to employ me during my off-duty hours. I was an announcer for the basketball team, as well as a referee/umpire for intramural games in several sports. All of which paid an extra 10 bucks here and there to supplement my $55 salary twice a month.

He also made sure that under the press table at the monthly boxing shows was a case of beer. The press corps included me and a photographer. It's not like news organizations around the world were sending staff writers. Najarian figured a case of beer helped us (and a few friends) do a better job of covering the events.

In short, Najarian was the professor who taught me how to live the best life possible in the military. He was a raconteur, a promoter, a coach, and a bon vivant. I learned from him constantly.

My first contact when I arrived at Atsugi, JO2 Burr, rotated out soon, but I was the first wave of replacements. Soon a veteran of six years in the Navy, JO2 John Hammond, arrived. He had done tours on two aircraft carriers in Vietnam, had been the voice of Far East Network in Taiwan (remember "Good Morning, Vietnam?") and was worldly in the ways of the Navy. We also added the legendary first black Senior Chief Journalist in Navy history, Richard Graddock, and a couple of others.

Hammond, Stone and I were the staff of the paper, primarily, while Graddock was pretty much the voice of diversity in a Navy that didn't have much. He regularly cranked out formula stories about young black men succeeding as aircraft mechanics, or other such jobs, in the Navy, which were sent to the then thriving black newspapers in inner cities across America like the L.A. *Sentinel* and Chicago *Defender*.

Since Graddock's writing skills were marginal, and his claim to fame was more about breaking barriers and not stories, he pretty much stayed away from the newspaper. All the better for us.

We also added a Photographer's Mate 2nd class (PH2) John Greenwood, which created a difficult situation for the rest of us. Greenwood was the senior enlisted man in the office before Graddock arrived, which meant he outranked the rest of us. Yet as a newspaper staff, each of us needed to assign him as the photographer to shoot pictures of events, which gave us work-related rank, if not real rank, over him.

Greenwood was a little too Old Navy for the rest of us, and he was flexing his rank one day by insisting we come in on a Saturday to clean the office. We were more Journalists than sailors, so that was a day that was destined not to go well. In my 20 years, I had developed a bit of a knack for sarcasm. Some would point to the many twists and turns in my nose to suggest my mouth was guilty of issuing checks my fighting skills couldn't pay off.

In the course of that Saturday morning, with Greenwood supervising what would be the only cleaning day in my 2 years in the PAO, I may have said a few things under my breath that might have been considered inappropriate, or insubordinate, or perhaps prone to inciting problems.

Next thing I knew, Greenwood was flying across the office and picking up my heavy Underwood Standard typewriter and trying to drop it in my lap. Or face – not sure where it was destined to land. But LT (JG) Jamieson saw the event, came running out of his office, and stopped the fracas. When we all shared our version of the events, Jamieson decided Greenwood did not fit in a small office like ours and transferred him to the Photo Lab. He spent the rest of his tour at Atsugi rotating back and forth to Vietnam.

We later got a much more amenable photographer, who worked out well and fit in great with the staff. And Graddock became the senior man in the office, eliminating the rub that was Greenwood.

What did I say to incur Greenwood's wrath? Not sure exactly, but the fact he lost his temper over some words does not speak well for his leadership skills. Or his lack of self-control, which cost him a cushy assignment and got him sent back to Vietnam on a regular basis.

There was one other event that involves fighting – not mine – that comes to mind.

Early in my tour, I availed myself of one of the Navy's free benefits, by enrolling in a Japanese language class. While my attempts to learn Spanish in high school and at Santa Monica City College were mostly ineffective, I was motivated to learn Japanese. While most of the bar girls knew enough English to entertain a sailor at night, if you could converse in her native language, the relationship moved to another level.

Several times in my first few months in Japan, armed with the basic sentence structure of the language and the knowledge that all verbs conjugate the same way – no irregular verbs like English – I would board a train to some destination city. And since all train stations were in the city center, surrounded by bars, pubs and restaurants, I'd put myself in situations where I needed to converse in Japanese.

I purchased and carried with me constantly, a Chisai Geebeeki (small dictionary) that translated common words from English to Japanese and vice versa. I learned that I was a Kaikun Shimbunkisha (phonetic spelling), which meant Navy newspaperman.

My knowledge of basic Japanese helped me form relationships with a number of Japanese bar girls. And since the girls were loyal and almost never switched employers, I could date girls from different bars. Here's what would normally happen, I might visit a bar early in the evening – closing time was 11:30 p.m. and curfew to the base was midnight – and talk to my friend. She might be entertaining a sailor who was buying "ladies' drinks" for inflated prices. She and I would chat in Japanese about meeting after closing time. That often meant that while the hopeful sailor who had spent a bundle was waiting outside the front of the bar, she'd slip out the back door and meet me. If you missed curfew at midnight, you needed to stay out until 6 a.m., which meant a friend's apartment was a necessity.

Unbeknownst to me, a couple of my regular friends from different bars got together and learned they were dating the same guy. Me. And I guess they weren't happy with that situation. One of them had become a particularly good friend since I gave her an electric blanket that I'd inherited from a departing sailor. And her tiny apartment was not insulated, so an electric blanket was a luxury that produced many nights of thanks.

One night I was walking down the back street toward one of the bars when I noticed a fracas outside. Two bar girls were fighting and a few dozen sailors and bar girls were watching. One of the Shore Patrolman who was watching – not breaking up mind you, since no U.S. military was involved – was an acquaintance. I asked him what was happening, and he explained the two girls were fighting over a sailor they were both dating. Then I got close enough to learn who the girls were, and realized it was me. The SP suggested there was nothing good that could come of my presence there. I made an early return to the base and stayed away from both of those bars for a few nights.

Sagami-Otsuka was home away from home for single sailors. There were all kinds of bars, ranging from tiny to large, from six seats and a mama-san to large enough to have Filipino or Korean bands playing American songs.

The Tiger Bar was my "home bar," consisting of six seats, room for another six or so to stand, and the mama-san served whisky and beer for 100 yen (about 25 cents – the Japanese currency was pegged at 360 yen to the dollar by law in those days).

Typically, we would hang out at Tiger Bar until we had been tuned up enough for the adventures that would follow. Tiger Bar Mama-san, was a friend to many of us. She was good enough to extend credit until payday and exchange money.

The Japanese currency was tied to the U.S. Dollar since the occupation after World War II – only 20 years earlier – although the U.S. military did not use U.S. currency. Instead there was a form of Monopoly money, called Military Payment Certificates (or MPCs). You could buy a limited amount of Yen before heading off base, but sometimes you might find yourself with the wrong type of money due to gambling losses, or too many drinks for bar girls. It helped to have a friendly Mama-san who would change money or float loans.

One day in late 1968 or early 1969, the U.S. decided to switch from MPCs to real American dollars, with no bill larger than a $20. And it was a classified decision, with everyone given about two days to change currency before the MPCs became worthless. The idea was to knock down the thriving business of illegal money changers.

Since I knew the Tiger Bar Mama-san likely had a stash of MPCs, and with Mr. Jamieson's unofficial permission, I took a long lunch and drove to her bar one afternoon. She lived in the back of the bar, and was surprised to see me at her door. But when I explained the situation, she was grateful and gave me her stash of MPCs (perhaps $400). I changed them into dollars with my own cash and returned them to her that night.

Our friendship bloomed after that and I had a lot of drinks on the Mama-san in the weeks that followed. Officially, what I did was illegal, since Japanese businesses weren't allowed to have MPCs. But she was a friend and I wanted to help her out.

She was the kind of friend who would make sure somebody took a drunken sailor back to base before he got in trouble.

Najarian, the athletic director who taught me so much, had been a teammate of a football coach named Mike Giddings in college. Giddings later coached as an assistant at USC, was head coach at Utah State, and was on the staff of the NFL division champion San Francisco 49ers in 1968.

One day Najarian called me with a story. He was bringing five members of the 49ers staff to Japan to put on football clinics for military players as well as the Japanese college teams we regularly played in goodwill games. Head coach Dick Nolan, plus Giddings, and fellow assistants Paul Wiggin, Jim Shofner and Ernie Zwahlein, were guests of the U.S. Navy.

I was invited to most of the events that were involved, including the clinics. I also took on the role of tour guide for a couple of coaches who wanted to explore the night life.

At the end of the visit, Giddings was going to fly to Osaka in Southern Japan. While at Utah State, he had hosted a Japanese college coach for a visit. That coach invited Giddings to be his guest coach in a spring exhibition all-star game.

Najarian and my boss, Mr. Jamieson, agreed that I should find a way to cover the event.

That meant a trip on the then famous and revolutionary Bullet Train. I wound up in the bar car – surprise – and watched as the speedometer climbed to more than 200 kilometers per hour – more than 100 miles per hour. Pour me another drink please.

The event in Osaka was as much as study of international goodwill as it was one of coaching techniques. But when Giddings' team won, he was tossed into the air by the players, as was the tradition. He later claimed it aggravated a sore back but was a career highlight.

After writing about it for *The Skywriter*, I wrote a version to send back to the states and sold it to *The San Francisco Chronicle,* along with a picture of Giddings being tossed into the air. The piece ran in the *Chronicle's* Sunday section, and I got a $50 check, which probably paid for my transportation to and from Osaka.

Giddings and I would stay in touch for decades to come. First came his last head coaching position, with The Hawaiians of the World Football League in the mid-1970s. He brought Najarian home from Japan to be his General Manager, and I spent a couple of days in training camp at UC Riverside with them before a game against the Southern California Sun, which had quarterback Pat Haden and running back Anthony Davis (both from USC).

After the WFL folded, Giddings formed a scouting service, and became a source of talent evaluation to a half dozen NFL teams (one in each division of the league). He became a reliable source for me prior to the NFL draft and when teams I covered might be considering a trade.

We stayed in touch until my newspaper career ended and he eventually retired.

I loved the culture in Japan, and was constantly learning things. My first New Year's Eve in Japan was memorable for a lot of reasons, including a few new customs.

I had met a girl from Tokyo when the San Francisco 49ers coaching staff had come to Atsugi for a couple of clinics and a few goodwill events. My new friend was involved in some way in one of those events.

And I was certainly seeking goodwill when she invited me to spend New Year's Eve with her in Tokyo.

What I thought would be my goodwill and hers were on slightly different paths, but they eventually intersected, although getting there tried my patience.

Yuki had a very small apartment somewhere near the flashy Shinjuku district, and when I arrived, she was ready to start her New Year's Eve routine. While I may have expected booze, food, booze, bed, booze – the traditional American routine for a man barely 21 years old – she had a different plan.

While I watched and kept her company, she started out by cleaning her apartment. I thought this was a little eccentric, but I was learning. Then we went out to a neighborhood noodles shop, where we met with three of her girlfriends. My Japanese was improving, but not enough to keep up with their fast-paced conversation.

Eventually, she explained that what we were doing was her way of ensuring a Good Luck Start for 1969. After eating, we left and went to her favorite little bar and had a couple of cocktails. Only a couple.

Then we had another mission: The giant Buddhist Shrine in Tokyo, where tens of thousands, maybe even hundreds of thousands, of Japanese went on major occasions like New Year's Eve. We stood in line several hours for our chance to ring the bell, one of the ultimate ways to insure good luck.

And if you thought I was impatient early in the evening, my weak effort at patience was severely tested by the Shrine visit.

Finally, we returned to her apartment at 2:30 in the morning, and we finally celebrated New Year's Eve in what I thought was the traditional way. I was exhausted the next morning when I took the train back to Atsugi NAS. At least I wasn't missing any bowl games on television, since the Japanese did not care about American College football and there was no Armed Forces Network television (just radio) in those days.

One of the most successful aspects of my time in the Navy at Atsugi was a little unofficial, off-the-books business I started along with my three fellow enlisted journalists. Like most young sailors, we lived paycheck-to-paycheck (1st and 15th of each month in those days), and often the last days before paydays were a little lean.

We decided that rather than borrow from others, we'd set up our own little in-office bank. We each put in $5 to start, for a bank of $20. We limited the operation to we four, and had a set of rules: You could only borrow up to 50% of the fund, and you had to pay back $6 for each $5 you borrowed.

We were all regular patrons, and our little fund grew over our two years together. When I cashed out to head home, my share was worth $200. That's a pretty fair return on investment. Slush Funds were illegal, of course, but by keeping it among ourselves, we stayed under the radar.

THE BATTLE OF OLONGAPO (1969)

The capital of all things Navy in the Far East in the 1960s was Subic Bay Naval Base, in the Philippine Islands. With a war-fighting effort that included half a million troops, the U.S. was seriously engaged in Vietnam. In addition to all those soldiers, marines, sailors and airmen on land in Vietnam, the U.S. Navy also had a major fleet offshore, which usually included a couple of aircraft carriers and the dozen or so support ships that accompanied each.

These carrier groups would be on station for 30 to 45 days at a time, sending war planes on attack and bombing missions to North Vietnam on a round-the-clock basis. At the end of those demanding deployments, the aircraft carriers and their support group would pull off station for a break at Subic Bay.

This may have been the largest Naval base in the world at the time, as the major hub of all things heading to and from Vietnam. It was also the major source of rest, relaxation and fun for the hard-working sailors.

As was true with virtually every U.S. base in the Far East in those days, a thriving town existed outside the base to entertain the sailors. This was Olongapo. And there should have been campaign ribbons for Olongapo, because it was a major stop on every Navy man's itinerary during the Vietnam era.

Olongapo was a village of bars and restaurants which catered to the needs of a sailor with more money than time. You could see to life's many needs at a reasonable price. The great Filipino beer, San Miguel, was a quarter a bottle. And the sum of a night's pleasures (booze, companionship, hotel room) might add up to no more than 10 bucks.

The Navy insisted throughout my time in uniform that ship movements were classified – and this makes good sense. Why would you want to advertise when an aircraft carrier and a dozen escort ships would be moving into a port? This information was confidential, yet every bar girl, hostess and hooker within 500 miles knew in advance when a carrier group was pulling into Subic, Sasebo or Yokosuka (in Japan), or any other port.

After all, bar owners had to be able to staff appropriately when a lot of customers would be arriving. If you didn't have a security clearance to learn about when a carrier was coming into town, just check with a bar girl.

Part of the military's plan to entertain the troops was a robust sports program, that included base football teams. Our team at NAS Atsugi, Japan, had several former college players – including a D-II quarterback – and we were capable of playing at a high level.

At the height of the Vietnam War, the Navy decided to send the Atsugi football team to the Philippines to play the Subic Bay team in some sort of Far East Championship. The powers that be in Japan decided I needed to accompany our team and write about this big game for *Stars and Stripes*, as well as our base newspaper.

Our civilian athletic director and football coach, George Najarian, rarely missed a trick, but he may have stumbled a bit when he decided to bring his team to the P.I. three days early to get accustomed to the tropical weather. That meant three nights of liberty in Olongapo for the football players and others.

Let me flash ahead to the Monday morning after the Sunday afternoon game: A Navy Corpsman was treating one of the traveling party when he explained the legend: "If you've been in Subic for one night you have a 1 in 3 chance; if you've been here two nights, the chances are 2 out of 3, and if you've been here three nights with three women, the chances are 100 percent that you have the clap."

That would be gonorrhea for those more medically inclined and it was the most prevalent venereal disease of that era. Easily treated by a massive shot of penicillin, it was still inconvenient.

And for a group of 40 football players struggling with extremely muggy tropical weather, and playing against a team that was their physical match in a close game, it might have sapped a little strength in the fourth quarter.

The bottom line was a victory for the home team from Subic, and a surprising loss for Atsugi. For many of us, there were also wagers with our counterparts from the home base, which hurt since we believed in our Atsugi Flyers a little too strongly. See later chapter on football gambling.

After the game, we were scheduled to stay over Sunday night before flying home. I was invited with Najarian and a couple of his coaches, who were officers, to drown our sorrows at the Officers' Club. In the course of our first 4 or 6 beers, we got into a debate with some of the pilots off whatever carrier was on break from Vietnam at the time.

As I recall, the debate was about music. In a classic scene from the old western movies, you suddenly had the four guys from Atsugi lined up across from the four pilots, in front of the juke box, and trading thoughts about music. Somebody threw the first punch – my amnesia is a matter of record – and suddenly eight grown men were grappling around, throwing punches and insults, all over a choice of songs on the jukebox.

These things aren't supposed to happen in the O Club, where gentlemen would go to relax. But after a miserable loss on the football field, somehow, they did. The mini-brawl was quickly broken up and we dusted ourselves off and got into a cab.

Before we could pull away, the Filipino bar manager came running out, waving something, and asking if there was a "petty officer second class Cox" in the car. Seems my ID card had fallen out in the fight. We grabbed the card and escaped to an off-base bar to continue licking our wounds.

Second class petty officers are enlisted men, a category that doesn't allow entrance into O Clubs, and for good reason. The rowdy lower class (enlisted men) might start a brawl or something similarly un-officer-like.

Monday morning, noticing possible symptoms, many in the traveling party visited the Infirmary, and learned from the Hospital Corpsmen that they needed a shot of penicillin before flying home. That, and perhaps a good story for the wife or lover about why there would be a five-day embargo on relations.

Years later, when NFL coaches insisted they wanted teams to spend the shortest amount of time in city before a game, I understood why.

NAVY IN JAPAN, WITH WIFE (1969-1970)

Every young sailor heard some version of this from a salty old chief when he was considering making "an adult decision" to get married: "If Mother Navy had wanted you to have a wife, she'd have issued you one when you got your sea bag in boot camp."

And while we may have appreciated the wisdom of those who have been with Mother Navy longer, there was also the feeling that we knew something about our own life. Such as deciding at midnight one night to make a long-distance phone call from Japan to the United States that would be considered rash, spur-of-the-moment, and maybe even immature. Like getting married to the girl you left behind over a year ago, had already cancelled previous wedding plans with, and all this while living in a place that was very friendly to single young men.

In keeping with a lifelong philosophy of "no regrets" – if you are noticing a trend here – I would never call it a mistake. Nor would I question my own lack of thinking on this move. Nevertheless, from the perspective of time, I can't help but ask the young me, "what were you thinking?"

After getting settled in Japan, and finding enjoyable the single life that included bars and bar girls, I was sent on a choice overseas trip in February 1969. I was asked to accompany our basketball team to Taiwan (Nationalist China, the one we recognized in those days). It was a 10-day trip and all I had to do was write a daily story for *Stars and Stripes,* the

Far East military newspaper, and a couple of stories and columns for our weekly base newspaper. And I was adding China – well, one version of it – to my list of countries visited.

When traveling with our sports teams, I was often treated as an officer, despite my enlisted status. That meant getting to participate in the unofficial Welcome to Taiwan party hosted by a navy dentist friend of our coach, Jimmy Powers, who was a dentist from the Boston area. He was the extra-duty officer assigned to coach the basketball team, when not extracting teeth.

There were maybe four of us, plus a couple of officers assigned to the Navy station on Taiwan. The local guy picked up bottles of 12-year-old Scotch (Johnny Walker Black) at the Navy Exchange which meant a price of about $2 a quart, and we rode taxis up into the foothills outside Taipei to a resort-like property. The mama-san showed us to our hospitality suite and food and girls started arriving right away. The girls arrived on mopeds or scooters and were part of a traveling group of high-end "hostesses" that worked the resort area. The party lasted until we were all maxed out on food, booze, and pleasure. As I recall, the tab might have been 20 dollars each.

As the basketball tournament unfolded over the next week, I learned a lot about night life in Taipei. Come to think of it, my mission during my time in the Navy and in the Far East was learning about the nightlife of Asian countries.

I learned about the contract system, where you bought a bar girl's services for the rest of the night, and the next day, for a modest amount. Perhaps $15. You signed a contract, and checked whether she was coming with you for dancing, dining, sightseeing or a few other innocuous events. When you checked into a hotel, the girl left her copy of the contract at the front desk. Since prostitution was controlled by the government (meaning regular inspections for disease, etc.) it was Taiwan's way of keeping track of the workers.

I kept a copy of that contract for the next 25 years as a memento, but it has since evaporated.

While I loved my Japanese female friends, I decided that Chinese women were special too. In those I days, I could fall in love with a town, a country, or a lifestyle in a week's visit.

When we returned to Japan, I was a little depressed. So, one night after having a few 25 cent cocktails during dinner on base because I had "the duty," I came back to the office and looked at the phone that connected to the Japanese phone system, not the on-base communications system. And before I could think of how stupid it was – or the time difference, for that matter – I had dialed Lorraine's family house and called collect. Her father answered, grudgingly accepted the charges, and put her on the line. One 70-dollar phone call later, I had wiped out a year of independence and nearly daily letters and agreed to come home in March to get married.

Never mind that Mother Navy had not issued me a wife – nor allowed me to have "an authorized wife," or the fact there would be some costs and logistical difficulties in pulling off this venture. Heck, I was 21 years old, and bullet-proof.

Getting home was easy. The U.S. military was running the world's largest airlift operation in those days, between CONUS (continental U.S.) and the Far East, where we were fighting a war in Vietnam. Most of the flights passed through Yokota Air Force Base in Japan, and all you needed was paperwork (orders) permitting you to go on leave for however many days (say 14 days). That got you on the standby list. This was pre-computer, so there were large chalkboard lists of flights arriving and departing from all over the Far East – usually the Philippines or Vietnam – and headed to "the world," which was military slang for the U.S.

I got a flight home within a few hours – it was an 8-hour direct flight – and within a week or so, Lorraine and me and our families had agreed to drive to Las Vegas and get married. But not all her family. Her father was not happy that his youngest daughter wasn't getting married in the Catholic church, so he skipped the trip.

I had a little problem with my family. Seems that my dad had taken ownership of my dress suits while I was gone, and he wanted to attend the wedding in my best suit. I wound up letting him have that one and I took another. The wedding was in one of those chapels that charge like a buffet line – $30 for the ceremony, $10 for a recording of it, $15 for flowers, $10 each for witnesses if you needed them, etc. And then we spent a few minutes celebrating, and we were back to our motel. A day later the wedding party was headed back to So Cal. And a few days later, we were headed to our new home in Japan.

That's when I learned that since Mother Navy did not issue my wife, there were a few hoops to jump through.

For starters, while I could fly back to Japan space-available (or standby) out of Travis AFB near Oakland, my new bride was not "an authorized wife," so she had to get to Japan by commercial air. I hadn't thought about that. There was also the matter of her needing permission from the Atsugi Commanding Officer to allow the unauthorized wife of a sailor at his base into the country.

None of this was in my pre-wedding planning. So, we flew to the Bay Area, and stayed in transient housing for military families, at Oakland Army base, while we tried to work these things out at Mare Island Navy base. Because it was a weekend, and because a previous president (Eisenhower) had died, there were non-working days for the military, and there were the seven time zones to consider. After 3 or 4 days of waiting, we had permission for Lorraine to come to Atsugi.

We took a bus to SFO, and bought a plane ticket for the next day on a flight to Tokyo on a Diners Club credit card that I had before joining the navy. Lorraine then went to some friends' house for the night, and planned to catch a flight to another part of the world without her husband of a few days. I caught a bus to Travis AFB and got on the waiting list. Only instead of a few hours – as it was coming to the States – it looked like days on the wait. I sent telegrams to my friend and editor on the base newspaper, John Hammond, and our interpreter, Koji Ishiwata, asking them to meet the Japan Air Lines Flight when it landed at Tokyo Airport and to pick up a redhead. And hoped for the best.

Telegrams: Perhaps I should explain that this primitive way of communication was all we had in the pre-cell phone, pre-text message, pre-email world. And you never knew when it was delivered, or received.

Lorraine's flight arrived, and John and his Japanese wife and Koji met the flight, and she went to spend her first night in Japan without her husband at the rural home of Hammond. Which had the Japanese style toilet that required squatting over the non-flush facility.

And I spent 30 hours moving around the various standby lists at Travis before a couple of near empty planes arrived and I got a flight to Japan.

I lived in a tiny apartment back then, with no bathing facilities, so first order of business was to find a newer, bigger, apartment. Although bigger applies to the two apartments, our spaces in Japan were tiny by American standards.

It had two rooms, divided by sliding doors, and covered in straw tatami mats. Our bedding (futon), folded up each night and went into the closet. There was a small kitchen, a toilet room (for our flush benjo, or toilet) and a room which held our Japanese-style bathtub. We did not have hot running water, so the water in the tub had to be heated for use, and both residents used the same water. You washed outside the tub, then rinsed in the hot water.

Our housing was a couple of miles off base, which meant you had to have a car, which I did, or take a military or civilian bus. We lived near a shopping area, but this was much different that shopping at Vons or Ralphs back home. So much was verbal, and in a language Lorraine did not understand.

Occasionally she would venture out and procure some food and try to prepare a meal. More often, we dined out either at the club on base or in small local restaurants.

We had a small black and white television, which picked up a few Tokyo stations – all in Japanese, again a language Lorraine did not understand. Armed Forces Network provided 24-hour a day programming on the AM radio, which was in a language she could understand.

But this was a challenge for a 21-year-old American woman and she was probably also wondering what she'd gotten herself into.

We had an active social life, but our friends with wives had all married Japanese women, who were learning English.

I tried to set up weekend and holiday events so that we could learn about the country and we drove into Tokyo or Yokohama a few times.

Navy guys tended to pass important items like cars down when it was time to rotate back to the States. I picked up a used Hillman for about $200 from another sailor. Nothing special about the car, although it was right-side drive, and seated four snugly.

On one of our adventures away from the base, I was driving on a Sunday on one of the many two-lane roads, and learned another lesson. I encountered a young Japanese motorcyclist who was trying to speed around me on the left or curb side. How we came in contact, I can only guess. But he wound up driving into a post, and wound up in the hospital with a broken leg and a few other injuries.

That's when I learned about the concept of "Gomen-nasai" money. That's a phonetic spelling for "I'm sorry," and in Japan, you often show you're sorry with an economic gift. In fact, my punishment in the Japanese court was based on whether I had followed the process. At the urging of our interpreter, Koji, I took the appropriate amount of money (maybe $100) and visited the motorcyclist in the hospital. I was sorry, and I showed it with my money.

One highlight was a visit to Japan by two photographer friends from the *Citizen-News,* Bob Martin and Jeff Goldwater. Lorraine still has pictures of the four of us playing golf one summer day in 1969 at Atsugi's course.

Martin was introduced to one of my Japanese friends, Emiko, who worked in the personnel office. She was a little older and more mature than I was – as was Martin – and the two of them wound up getting married and she moved to Southern California.

Goldwater wound up marrying Lorraine a very short time after our divorce became final, and she had two additional children with him. That short visit by the two photographers back in 1969 turned out to have lasting meaning for Jeff and Lorraine

A major event that rattled all of us in the Atsugi community occurred later that year. One of the giant Constellation planes that our surveillance squadron (VQ-1) flew was shot down by the North Koreans. All on board were lost, and fortunately none were friends, although I did have a close friend in that squadron.

The news of that event became international when it was learned that many of those on the plane were soldiers from the nearby Army base at Camp Zama and their military occupational specialty (MOS) was Chinese Language.

Officially, we were monitoring the weather in the area between China, and North Korea, however worldwide speculation was a little more sinister.

Our base became a hub for international news for a week or so, including the memorial service and discussion about what U.S. Navy planes were doing flying these types of missions from a base in Japan. Our role in Public Affairs was to assist the visiting journalists.

I remember escorting one reporter from the *New York Times* around our base, and trying to answer some of his questions. I was unable to explain why we used a herd of goats to mow the grass that covered a field of buried storage areas. Chances are we had serious weaponry in those bunkers, and goats were less likely to set off weapons than power mowers, but that was purely speculation. For once in my life, I was towing the party line and gave only approved answers.

We also made international news that year when one of our helicopter pilots, LT Clyde Lassen, received the Medal of Honor for a daring rescue of a downed pilot in North Vietnam. We all got to write stories about his heroic mission and got to know LT Lassen. Since he was a living Medal of Honor winner, he was a celebrity for the rest of his Naval career.

Mostly our time in Japan was more mundane.

A month after we got to Japan, the Navy informed me I had passed the test for Second Class Petty officer (E-5) and that meant not only more money, more allowances, but also meant I was responsible enough to have a wife. But since she was here unofficially, and I would have needed to add nearly two years to my enlistment to make her authorized, she remained unofficial.

That meant when it was time to return to the States – in 1970 – I would have to give up my reserved seat to fly standby, again, with Lorraine. Only this was the time when the U.S. started drawing down our troop presence in the Far East. We wound up spending five days on the plastic seats in the air terminal at Yokota AFB before catching a flight home. That was five days in my dress blues – scratchy wool uniform – and I wound up in a center seat on a 707. I slept the 8 hours across the Pacific.

When we got home, Lorraine and I were staying at her sister's apartment, and we did what a couple of 20-somethings did after 5 days in an airport. We slept. We made love. And we repeated the process for several days.

A few months later, I learned that since we were not participating in the second part of that equation while in the airport in Japan, Lorraine saw no need to take her birth control pills.

Hello Lisa.

Now our adventurous young marriage was taking a few more turns, with parenthood looming at the age of 22.

Lorraine and I managed to grow apart for another four years before figuring out this was a marriage that probably wasn't working. So, in the end I realized there was some wisdom in the old Navy saying about a wife being issued.

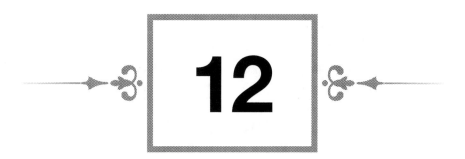

BACK TO THE REAL WORLD (1970)

The United States' involvement in Vietnam, which had peaked at more than half million men (and women) in the late 1960s, was suddenly ebbing as the '70s began. We were pulling out, and because of that, the military didn't need as many troops. So, while buildups and waivers of time in grade for promotions were common a year earlier, there suddenly was a rush to trim the ranks.

"Early outs" were being offered and unless you worked in a field where there were serious shortages (technical skills, for example), the chance to go home early was suddenly available. While I had signed a couple of extensions to get the assignment in Japan and two promotions, I was suddenly offered the chance to wipe them off the book. Instead of serving until June, I was given the chance to leave active duty in February 1970.

While there was a perceived shortage of mid-level (E-5) Journalists only a year earlier, suddenly there was a surplus. The Navy's presence in the South China Sea, or the Tonkin Gulf Boat Club as it was occasionally called, was being reduced. Fewer ships requiring fewer journalists, fewer units "in country" similarly requiring fewer journalists, created a ripple effect. Someone in the Navy Personnel Department in D.C. had determined a number of enlisted men and women would be offered a chance to go home early.

I was one of them. And while I loved Japan as a single man, and truly appreciated the adventures of traveling around that country, plus the Philippines and Taiwan, it was not the same as a married man with an American wife. While she was a trooper to the end, I knew Lorraine pretty much hated living in Japan. She had few American female friends and since we lived off base in the local economy, she had few opportunities to spend time with other American dependents. So, if there was any doubt as to whether I'd be accepting the "early out," Lorraine was clear – turning it down was not an option.

I had occasionally pondered the idea of sticking around the Navy for a career. I had risen quickly to E-5 (Journalist 2nd Class) and figured I could get to Chief Journalist (E-7) pretty quickly as well. Then I'd be in charge of a group of journalists, or the top enlisted man in a public affairs office. But there was one snag in my thinking. To make Chief Journalist, I'd have to spend at least one assignment of two years at sea. Journalists weren't assigned to small boats, so that meant an aircraft carrier or cruiser. But it still meant 30 or 60 days at sea at a time. Long periods of duty on a ship. While my main job as a journalist was still in the field I'd trained, I would also have collateral duties on various disaster teams. My source was buddy John Hammond, also a JO2, who had served tours on two different carriers. He had been on a firefighting crew (as a hose man, whatever that is) and actually had to fight a couple of fires on the *Bon Homme Richard* (AKA the Bonnie Dick, one of the great nicknames in the Navy).

And since I had been cultivating my appreciation for bottled spirits – and there was no drinking on those 30 or 60-day cruises – that would put a serious crimp in my budding career as an alcoholic. So, sticking around for another enlistment of four years – or even turning down the "early out" and staying 'til summer, was not a viable option.

Normally when a sailor leaves his overseas assignment, he gets a guaranteed seat on a charter airliner bound for the Real World, or CONUS (Continental United States). But because I had brought Lorraine to Japan as an unauthorized dependent, I could only return with her on a space-available status. So, on a wintry February day, we were dropped off at Yokota Air Base to await two seats on a plane bound for the U.S. Unlike my previous Space-A travels from Japan to the U.S. and from Travis AFB to Japan, this one was coming during the greatest Rush Hour in trans-Pacific travel in years. Tens of thousands of U.S. servicemen were filing every seat on the charter planes headed home from Vietnam, the Philippines, Korea, Okinawa, and Japan.

So, we took our place well down the Space-A list and pulled up a couple chairs to wait in the spartan lounge at Yokota. I was in my wool Navy dress blues which seemed appropriate for the winter. Five days later, I suspect the wool had gotten a little ripe. Anyway, in the evening of the fifth day, after finding every way possible to kill time, we finally boarded a plane. I wound up in a middle seat – something I would later spend a lifetime avoiding – and I was so tired I hardly noticed since I slept for most of the eight hours across the Pacific.

After landing at Travis AFB, outside the Bay Area, we were bused to SFO, where we caught a commuter flight to LAX and a reunion with the families.

A few hours of partying later, we did what two 20-something married kids who had just spent five days in an airport lounge might be expected to do. We slept for 48 hours, intermingled with a little conjugal bliss.

There was the formal matter of separation from active duty, which had to be accomplished at the Long Beach Naval Base. I drove down there on a Monday morning, and started the process. Which was more waiting around and processing paperwork than anything else. There was a separation physical, and final pay accounting, and my official transfer to the Naval Reserves and the Santa Monica Station where it had all begun with my enlistment. This took several days. I was assigned a bunk at Long Beach, but because of my status as an E-5, I was allowed to go home at night.

There was one close call, where my careful negotiation around the military requirements of becoming a 2nd Class Petty Officer nearly came back to haunt me. Although all of us waiting for processing were technically in a duty status, we were mostly killing time. But an occasional assignment came up that had to be filled. Towards liberty call (4:30 p.m.) of my second day in this transit status, the chief in charge of the group said they needed a couple of volunteers for Shore Patrol duty in Long Beach. The requirement was to be a 2nd class Petty Officer, since you'd be assigned a hand gun, the military version of the Colt 45. Fortunately, a couple of guys who were spending time in the transit barracks volunteered. Had I been assigned, it might have become apparent that while my service record indicated I was capable to carrying, firing, and field stripping a .45, as was the requirement to advance to my current rank, I had never even held a 45. One of my drinking buddies at Atsugi was the master at arms and he had previously signed off on my competency with the weapon, feeling assured that I'd never be asked to prove it.

CIVILIAN LIFE (1970-74)

After separation from the Navy, I had two weeks to decide whether to return to the *Citizen-News*, the paper in Hollywood where it all started for me. Or try something else. I had flown to Miami for a three-day interview/tryout on the news and sports desks of the Miami *Herald*. At the end, I was not offered a position. Once again, it turns out that was the best thing possible. Another So Cal journalist who went to Miami spent 25 years trying to get back.

So, I went back to the *Citizen-News* and started working on the news desk, and in a whirlwind of different jobs in a few months, including copy editor, entertainment writer, news editor, City Hall reporter, and eventually City Editor. This covered the span of about March through August of 1970.

About the same time, we learned that Lorraine was pregnant, which complicated life just a little.

This was a bad time for newspapers in America – or maybe it was the beginning of the bad times which have continued to this day – but papers were folding. One was the *Citizen-News*. But not without a lot of laughs and some great moments.

During my stint in entertainment, we were invited to Lake Tahoe for the opening of a Burt Bacharach show at Harrah's. I knew nothing about music, or how to review a show, but it was a weekend freebie, and that mattered. It was during a winning streak at the blackjack table at Harrah's that Lorraine passed out. We thought it was the altitude, but later learned that was the first sign of her pregnancy.

I was a City Hall reporter for only a couple of weeks, but I got the full indoctrination. I was introduced to the veteran president of the Los Angeles City Council, John Gibson, and he presented me with my very own key to the executive restroom. The Councilmen, their aides, and the newspaper guys shared a restroom that required a key to enter. Years later, you wonder, what would they have done had there been any female reporters, or council persons. It was a moot point, in those days.

J. Michael Kenyon arrived from Seattle, and quickly took over as Managing Editor – he was older at perhaps 28 or 30 – and we hired a bright young reporter named Bella Stumbo, later to earn national acclaim at the L.A. *Times*. We three, working under a former TV newscaster from Detroit named Phillip Nye, were given a newspaper to play with in that heady summer of 1970. Unfortunately, the reason the kids were turned loose was because ownership, heirs of the famed Du Pont family, was losing its shirt. It was hard to sell a newspaper that operated out of an aging plant with a dying circulation base in an area in transition.

That Summer of 1970 was an eye-opener for me. Following the lead of Kenyon and Stumbo, we became a very liberal paper. Major stories on the Gay Rights movement, which was just evolving. The first-ever Gay Rights Parade was on Hollywood Boulevard, just a few blocks from our office. We all went and walked alongside the marchers.

There was also another event that summer which probably said a lot about my future in the marriage with Lorraine.

One of our female reporters was dating a guy who was the Mayor of Burbank, so many on our staff were invited to a party. Lorraine was maybe 6 months into her pregnancy with Lisa. At that party, I was enjoying the cocktails and hanging out with reporters and young and vibrant politicians.

Somewhere in the course of the evening, many of us wound up in a spare bedroom, sitting on the floor in a circle, passing around a joint. This was at a time when marijuana was illegal. Lorraine wandered into the room and wondered what was going on. When she figured it out, she was upset, and wanted to go home. I was enjoying the party, and she wound up getting a ride home with one of our staffers. I spent the night on a couch and came home the next morning.

As summer progressed, the ownership group (an heir to the DuPont fortune) stopped making payroll. So, every Wednesday (payday), the publisher would put a couple of bottles of liquor on the desk and give a pep talk. Many of us vowed to work another week. And some left each week. We wound up working six weeks without pay before the paper finally folded.

My youthful naivete prevented me from worrying. There was unemployment insurance, perhaps $80 a week. That got us the rent and we ran up a sizeable credit card debt along the way. I had a couple of courtesy interviews, but the bottom line was there were no newspaper jobs, either in SoCal or anywhere else.

Finally, about October, I realized there was a kid on the way, and I needed have a job. So, I took the test to see if I could become an insurance salesman. This was the easiest test I've ever taken. They had 300 questions, all asking if you were gregarious and enjoyed talking to people, or preferred being alone. I was offered a job and began training. After two weeks of training, Lorraine went into labor on the weekend, and Lisa was born on a Sunday. On Monday morning, I bought a handful of cheap cigars, went into the office of the insurance company and handed them to my bosses and fellow trainees.

Then I quit.

"I've been fooling myself and you guys," I told them. "As soon as a newspaper job opens up, I'll be gone."

Besides, while toasting the birth of my child in a lonely apartment in North Hollywood on Sunday night, I realized the hidden truth of the matter. The hospital wasn't going to repossess the baby, whether we paid our bills or not.

Within a week, I had two job offers, one as managing editor of a weekly paper called the San Fernando *Sun*, and one on the sports staff of the *Daily Breeze* in Torrance. I accepted the San Fernando job on Thursday and was supposed to start on Monday. Sports Editor Mike Waldner of the *Breeze* offered me that job on Friday morning and asked if I could start work that night. I accepted and worked Friday and Saturday nights. Then Monday morning I called the San Fernando *Sun* and burned that bridge. The *Breeze* gig worked pretty well – I lasted 27½ years until taking an early retirement in 1998 to go into education.

Life at the Breeze in the 1970s was a great ride. I was the weekend "slot man" or section editor, working on Friday and Saturday nights. I also had two "beats" to cover, which got me out of the office occasionally. I covered auto racing and boxing. Neither was a particular favorite of mine, but I took possession of each and owned them as much as possible.

At one time, I figured out that each involved athletes pushing the life or death button and taking serious chances. That brought a lot of women to these events. Auto racing involved a half dozen major events a year at Riverside and Ontario Raceways.

Auto racing usually involved a long day driving and covering, but on rare occasions, I was allowed to stay over after covering the Saturday events. One moment strikes a memory: Sitting at a bar where race fans hung out, I was chatting with a young lady, when she grabbed my hands and checked out my fingernails. "You're not a driver or crewman," she said after noted my clean nails. "I'm a writer," was my feeble response as she started looking for somebody with closer ties to the sport.

Boxing was in a great growth period in Southern California in the early 1970s. There were weekly cards at the Olympic Auditorium on Thursday nights. The Forum wanted to get into the action, and started holding Monday night events. There were also periodic major world championship fights, some at the Forum, some at the Coliseum and at the Sports Arena.

There were major stars among the lighter weights, including Jose Napoles, Mando Ramos, Indian Red and Little Red Lopez, among others. The heavyweights had also become big business with fights in Las Vegas or other exotic locales, but Muhammad Ali and promoter Bob Arum would occasionally come to town to promote an event.

I enjoyed meeting the auto racing drivers and writing their stories but watching the races was not my favorite activity. Although I got to attend 3 Indy 500s and the early Long Beach Grand Prix events among major races, it should be noted that I have not attended an auto race in person since leaving the beat. Nor have I watched on television.

I liked boxing better than auto racing but again, I've never attended a fight I wasn't paid to attend.

After taking the job at the Breeze late in 1970, Lorraine and I moved into an apartment on Paseo de la Playa in Redondo Beach. We enjoyed being less than a block from the beach. Because much of my work was at night, I had my days to play volleyball.

Dan McLean and I became friends in the 1960s while covering the Dodgers. The *Breeze* seat in the Dodger Stadium press box was next to the *Citizen-News* spot, and we enjoyed chatting during games. While I was in the Navy in Japan, Dan, who was born in Canada, moved to Montreal for a couple of years to cover the Expos. He returned to SoCal and we spent a lot of time playing beach volleyball before he was re-hired by the *Breeze*.

McLean and a neighbor of ours, Bobbi McLaggen, were among the regulars at our apartment for beers and parties.

Although work was great, I realized that not having a college degree was a potential impediment to my future, and since the wonderful GI Bill was willing to pay something like $300 a month for me to attend college, I parlayed my night-time working assignments into attending classes during the day.

It took about three years at El Camino College to earn an associate's degree and that happened only after a female sports stringer who was also attending ECC agreed to take a biology class with me under an important agreement: She did all the dissecting, and I wrote all the papers. I wanted nothing to do with those frogs.

I moved on to Cal State Dominguez Hills and attended school until the GI Bill funding ran out. While I had more than enough units to graduate, they didn't add up to a degree. I had changed majors regularly at CSUDH, from English to History to Sociology to American Studies. I'd find a class I liked that was taught by a hot professor – usually a female although hot could also describe a bright and interesting male professor, such as Sociology guru Hal Charnofsky, a onetime Yankee minor league infielder. I took enough sociology classes during that phase of my infatuation to wind up with it as my eventual minor.

In 1973, I kept a promise to Lorraine and we moved off the beach and into our first house, in North Redondo. Again, thanks to the GI Bill, we were able to buy a house with no down payment. The smallish 2-bedroom, plus den, and 1 bath, sold for $29,500.

About 15 years later, when Nancy and I were looking for a house, that same corner house on Spreckels Lane was selling for $300,000, 10 times what we paid.

I remember filling out the paperwork and noticing the loan went for 360 months (30 years) and asking what if I wanted to take off and sail to Tahiti?

As it turns out, I have since had more than a dozen 30-year loans and have never paid off any of them. Of course I've never sailed to Tahiti, either. But it's always in the back of my mind.

Lorraine and I lived in that house for about a year.

I met a lot of young women during my extended trek through academia, and that didn't help the home life. Lorraine and I were gradually growing apart, which is not surprising since we were 21 years old when we got married, and we each had some growing up to do.

Bottom line, we grew apart and Lorraine and 4-year-old Lisa finally moved back to her family homestead in Glendale. And in November of 1974, Lorraine filed for divorce and I was required to pay $175 per month in child support.

I later challenged that over a small issue. I wanted Lisa to take swimming lessons during her weeklong visit with me, but Lorraine did not want the cost ($40 as I remember) to come out of the monthly amount of child support. I checked with my attorney, who said, "Bob, if this goes back to court, three things will happen: You'll lose on asking her to pay for the lessons, you'll pay both attorneys' fees, and the judge will raise the amount you're paying."

A day later, I paid Lorraine everything I owed and sucked up the cost of the swimming lessons on my own.

While my return to civilian life was marked by marriage, fatherhood and newspaper work, I was still technically a member of the Naval Reserve for another three years. The initial enlistment of six years included two more "active reserve" years, plus a final year on the inactive roster.

Active reserve meant attending a meeting four Tuesday nights a month, or one weekend meeting every month. We were paid depending on rank, and I might have been getting 20 bucks a meeting.

But shortly after my return, I met the commanding officer of the station, and he felt there was a need for a monthly newspaper. We quickly worked out a compromise: I would put out a four-page mimeographed newspaper ever month in lieu of attending four meetings. I would still get credit for the meetings and pay. I just needed to come by and pick up the articles or news he wanted covered, and put out the paper.

Once again, my journalism skills were setting me up with a good deal. At the end of my two-year stint, the commander wanted me to stick around another year, but I declined, and separated from the Navy.

FIRST DAUGHTER: LISA (1970-PRESENT)

Through no fault of her own, Lisa got me as the absentee dad for most of her formative years.

She was about 4 when Lorraine and I split up, and my presence in her life for the next 14 years was spotty, at best. There would be some big moments but there would also be great gaps.

I was too busy growing up on my own to spend much time in the parental role. No excuses. I was selfish.

We did have some fun memories, including a flight to Mammoth on a small plane when she was about 6; a trip to Washington, D.C., and a visit to the White House; a long weekend in Big Bear for a pro ski race when she was able to hang out with the racers at about 16, and a trip to Hawaii.

Credit for great parenting goes to Lorraine and Jeff, who she married shortly after our divorce. Their family also included two other children, so Lisa had siblings and a stable home life.

When Lisa got to high school, at Reseda, and it was apparent she was a talented student, I did jump into the picture and start motivating her with visions of college options. Nancy and I took her on tours of a half dozen UC campuses, including UC Santa Barbara, which was her final choice.

My message through her high school years was simple: If you get the grades to get into a four-year school, I'll handle the costs.

While Lorraine may have wondered how that could be true, I was hitting my prime as a football writer about that time, and had every outside writing gig available. I was the correspondent, or stringer, for Sports Illustrated, The Associated Press, and The Sporting News. That extra income was a major factor in funding four years at UCSB.

Lisa and I grew close during the pre-college process and were probably at our closest during her four years at Santa Barbara.

That started with a three-day trip to the campus in the summer for an orientation weekend, and included trips to secure housing. For reasons I don't remember, Lisa did not get into the major freshman housing complex, and we wound up having to get her a share of a 5-person suite at a private apartment complex. That created some learning experiences when her roommates were not very good about making utilities payments, but she survived.

By her final two years, Lisa was in a small apartment with one roommate and was thriving in her independent living.

College was a great experience for her and I remain proud of her for qualifying for one of the top schools in the UC system, and graduating in four years.

She also learned much about the working world with part-time jobs, mostly at Subway.

My memories of her four years at UCSB including a number of Saturday trips in which we mostly got to know more about one another. She'd share with me her experiences and I'd try to relate them to the real world.

During her first year at UCSB, Lisa and her mother had some sort of tiff, likely related to Lorraine and Jeff leaving the family home in Reseda and moving to Palmdale in the Antelope Valley. They were probably not wild about her going away to college.

Whatever the details, for the summer after her first year of college, Lisa came to Redondo Beach and moved in with Nancy and me. She also got a couple of jobs at retail stores in Torrance. It was a great summer.

She and Lorraine were back on great terms the next year, and as she progressed through UCSB, she decided she would move to Palmdale after graduation.

Her marriage to Nat Bulsombut was a source of great pride to all aspects of the family, and when she told me how she wanted Jeff and I to handle different roles in the ceremony, I was proud of her maturity and her ability to handle a tough situation.

Lisa and Nat soon found a home in Palmdale, not far from Lorraine and Jeff's place, and raised daughters Sydney and Sabrina, along with a lot of dogs, and cats. Lisa became known for her work with the PTA and was president for a number of years, receiving an award at one point.

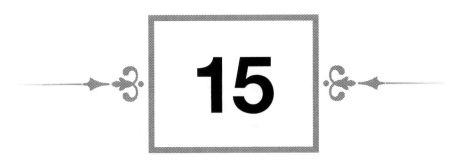

THE EARLY BREEZE YEARS (1970S)

When I was hired by the *Daily Breeze* in December of 1970 – rescued from my self-imposed exile in the world of life insurance sales – I was hired primarily for my skills as an editor.

My early training and the best advice I got from the old-timers at the Hollywood *Citizen-News* included the nugget that writers were a dime a dozen and editors were hard to find and coveted. Although most newspaper sports staff jobs in those days included a mix of writing and editing, it was the ability to design and package a sports section, along with the skills to edit a story, that secured the position.

My main job for most of the next six or seven years was to manage the sports section on Friday and Saturday nights, putting out the sections for the Saturday paper (heavy on high school sports) and the largest section of the week on Sunday.

But this did not mean a complete departure from writing. On a small sports staff, everyone got to do some writing. My "beats" were auto racing and boxing, two sports I would never have chosen, but that got me out of the office occasionally. But I made the best of those sports.

The boxing beat led me to covering 347 fights at the Olympic Games in 1984. Why 347? That happened to be the total of preliminary and final bouts in all weight classes that year. These were the Los Angeles Games, and since we had boycotted Moscow four years earlier, the Communist Bloc stayed away from L.A. That meant no Cuban, Russian or Romanian fighters were competing, and led to a near sweep of gold medals by American boxers. That also meant the daily boxing stories were nearly always on page one of the combined sports sections we produced for all the Copley Newspapers.

It also meant traveling to the Olympic boxing elimination events in Las Vegas and Fort Worth, Texas. It also means meeting Mike Tyson after he lost in the finals of the U.S. team selection process to an L.A. area hood named James Tillman, who won the Olympic gold that year, fought briefly as a pro, then went back to prison.

Boxing was good for me in the Summers of the mid-1970s because it was thriving in Los Angeles. Weekly fight nights on Thursdays at the Olympic Auditorium in downtown L.A., and on Monday nights at the Forum in Inglewood.

I never loved boxing, but I got pretty good at cultivating sources and became skilled at writing about it. Also included were a handful of World Championship fights, including a lightweight battle at the Coliseum featuring Mando Ramos.

I met Cassius Clay before he became Muhammad Ali, plus promoters like Don King and Bob Arum.

Auto racing was also thriving in those days. There were two major tracks in So Cal. Riverside International Raceway and Ontario Motor Speedway. There were also events several nights a week at Ascot Park, located near Gardena in the Breeze circulation area.

The promoters of auto racing were constantly striving to find ways to break into the daily newspapers, which were dominated by the big three (baseball, football, basketball) and which were yet to embrace hockey (until Wayne Gretzky joined the Kings). They were innovative and often came up with fun ideas that writers would rarely turn down.

Riverside International Raceway was a sprawling road course located where a shopping center now resides at the juncture of a couple of freeways. It hosted a lot of major races, but was hard to get to for many of us, and promoting auto racing was a challenge.

One year, before one of the stock car races, they offered a handful of writers the chance to ride in a race car and see the track at racing speeds. Stock cars were a natural for this, since they had a space where a passenger seat could be placed next to the driver. This would have been the early to mid-1970s, and Herschel McGriff of Oregon was one of the West Coast's top drivers, who regularly challenged the good old boys from the south in NASCAR events. He was in Riverside the week before the race to help promote it.

I arrived on a weekday and got my racing suit and helmet and was inserted into the car through the side window. Remember that all doors are welded shut, and window glass is removed from the side windows. I was buckled, strapped and snapped into place. And while I tried to start a conversation with McGriff, the noise level prevents anything but shouting.

We took off around the 2½ mile road course track at speeds quickly exceeding 100 miles per hour. On the straightaways, we probably went 160 miles per hour. This sheer speed – the fastest I'd ever traveled on ground – was not what got my attention. Frankly, the difference between 100 miles an hour and 150 or 160 on a straightaway is not as noticeable as you'd think.

What got my attention was heading into the turns and dropping down from that top speed of 160 to perhaps 90 or 100 to make a turn, in a couple of quick down shifts. This is happening with the empty grandstands seemingly dead ahead of us and on a collision course that would seem inevitable. McGriff shifted gears, tapped the brakes, and leaned into the turn at maybe 90 mph and it was all one smooth move for the veteran driver. It was the scariest moment I'd ever experienced on wheels.

Another race, another track, another PR Stunt.

That was to promote a major Indy-style open-wheeled racing event at Ontario Motor Speedway, which was a copy of Indianapolis Motor Speedway and offered seating for nearly 300,000 fans around a 2½-mile high-banked oval track. Parnelli Jones, the former Indy winner from Torrance and a local entrepreneur, was among the investors in this track.

To promote the upcoming race, they took the open-wheeled, low-slung race car that Mario Andretti had used to set the then closed-course speed record of something like 214 miles per hour and made a slight modification. They took out the engine that cost perhaps $40,000 to build and replaced it with a stock Chevrolet model that fit in the regular economy cars for sale at the time. Same size engine. Perhaps one fifth the horsepower.

But unlike the ride at Riverside, the select members of the motoring press would be driving this spectacular car albeit with the pedestrian engine. Again, we were outfitted in Simpson safety suits and racing helmets and googles. Fitting into the tight cockpit was a challenge since it was customized for a smallish man like Andretti, who was perhaps 5-foot-4 and 130 pounds.

But once in, with the engine running, and the tiny gear shift lever and even tinier gas and brake pedals explained, we were told we could drive as fast as we were comfortable for one lap.

Now since Ontario had high banked sides and turns, this seemed safe. I vowed to go as fast as the car and track would let me. While blasting down the back straight, I was impressed with myself, knowing I was going pretty fast. Surely well in excess of 100 miles per hour at a time when the speed limit on California Freeways was 55 miles per hour. But my satisfaction was dimmed a little when, driving as fast as the fastest car in racing would allow, I looked over my right shoulder and saw the safety truck that was accompanying me was holding its spot right behind me. Yeah, I was going 100 miles per hour on a fast track in the fastest car in existence but so was a tow truck.

It was exhilarating, and made for a fun story. But only after I took more than an hour to drive the afternoon freeways back to the office in Torrance at 55 miles per hour.

Ski racing got me a chance to experience speed in different ways in the 1970s.

The U.S. Pro Tour was a poor man's after-World Cup refuge for top racers who weren't ready to give up the sport yet. I was hanging out with the race crew when I was introduced to a former Canadian downhiller named Jungle Jim Hunter. He was looking for a tour of Mammoth Mountain, and I was appointed. We rode up to the top of the mountain, then Hunter wanted to take a rocket run down to the bottom, where the race course was being constructed.

I figured I could hang with him for a while, before remembering that downhillers are not like the rest of us. Going 70 or 80 miles an hour on skis is not a normal experience. He took off, blasted through ungroomed snow at speeds I could not imagine, and was waiting at the bottom relaxing when I came huffing and puffing along a minute or two later.

I did get to experience a different kind of speed on the snow later in the 1970s when the Camel Speed Tour arrived for a short, timed speed run. This required a helmet, borrowed from one of my Race Department buddies, and many raced on downhill skis, which were 240 centimeters long and very stiff. I did not have downhills, but raced on 218-cm giant slalom skis.

In this type of racing – popular for only a short time in the 70s and 80s, you got into a tuck position at the top of a long, straight run, and held it for about a mile, long enough to trip the speed gun.

I'd done a lot of what we thought were high-speed runs at Mammoth while free skiing, although we probably never went much faster than 30 miles an hour. As the Camel Tour event progressed, the course lengthened, allowing for higher speeds.

On one of my early runs, I was not able to hold my tuck all the way across the finish line, and by partially standing, I nearly blew up and crashed. I was able to hold it, but that didn't hold off the nightmares about that possible crash.

In my best run, I got to 65 miles an hour, which was 10 miles per hour faster than the California speed limit at the time. But after that bobble on a practice run on Friday, and the ensuing nightmares, I went to the registration desk on Saturday and turned in my bib. That was fast enough for me. I wrote about it in my weekly ski column that week.

Later I would experience the Super Giant Slalom course set by the World Cup tour at Mammoth in 1993, which went from the top of the mountain all the way to the Main Lodge. World Cup racers are on another planet from the rest of us, and they like their snow icy, slick and hard. As part of the press contingent, I was taken on a pre-race tour, and found the runs I usually traveled with ease totally terrifying. Mammoth's Cornice Bowl with soft snow is steep and challenging but fun. On a sheet of ice, it doesn't matter how sharp the edges of your skis, they are not sharp enough to hold.

Later, I learned that one of the Race Department coaches blew out a knee while side-slipping the ice patch. And our weekend club racers tried to manage the hard and fast training hill used by the slalom racers, and most could not negotiate the course.

ON THE ROAD: WENDOVER, UTAH (1972)

One of the promoters I met while covering the auto racing beat was a P.R. guy named Deke Houlgate.

Houlgate convinced my boss, Mike Waldner, to let me come along for the world speed record attempt by a South Bay driver named Gary Gabelich, who was more a drag racer than a track racer. He was willing to risk major injury to life and limb for a chance at fleeting fame.

Houlgate was promoting the automotive additive STP, which was sponsoring a run for the world land speed record. These are accomplished in vehicles that are more like rockets than cars, and there aren't a lot of places in the world where you can go 600 plus miles per hour.

One in fact.

That would be the Bonnevile Salt Flats in western Utah, near the Nevada line.

And to get press coverage of these type of news events, you often had to find a way to get the press to your event. In this case, there was a charter plane from Los Angeles for a 4-day adventure on the Flats.

There is nothing near the Bonneville Salt Flats, except wilderness. Very flat wilderness. There is a wide spot in the road called Wendover, Utah, which had a couple of motels and not much else. Except at its most western point, where it became Nevada, and there was a casino.

While watching a guy strapped into a land-based rocket for a streak across the desert may not have tickled my imagination, when I learned about the casino, the trip was looking better.

There were perhaps 100 folks from all stretches of the sports and automotive racing arenas on the charter plane for Utah and many had been through these events in the past.

There is a lot of down time as crews prepare the wheeled rocket for the speed run, and battle weather and wind.

Each night after the time in the desert, there would be a BBQ and time to hang out.

On our second night, one of the broadcast cameramen asked me if I wanted to join him and a couple of other old hands for a trip to Wells, Nevada. I had never heard of Wells, so couldn't imagine why. He explained that Wells was located in one of two counties in Nevada with legalized prostitution in those days. I was in.

We drove about 45 minutes to another small nothing town, but there was something unusual. There were two houses with neon signs on the roof. One was Ida's Place. I forget the name on the other house.

When we showed up at Ida's and were greeted by the hostess, the three guys who had done this before quickly took up spots at the bar. Since I had never been to a House of Prostitution, legal or illegal, I was a little slow. When the parade of four women came out to greet their new customers, I was slow in checking out my options. Until my option was the one young lady left after the three guys who knew what they were doing made their choices.

I don't remember the price, or much else, except that we went to her room and talked while I got my 24-year-old nerve up. Not that I was shy about these kinds of matters. I had spent two years in Japan, Taiwan and the Philippines. But I'd never gone through something like this without first getting well juiced.

When It was over and we were driving back through the wilderness to Wendover, the cameramen bragged about taking these assignments just so they could visit Ida's. And while my experience was not the most romantic, I did think that it was an important experience for the book that was many decades down the road.

I knew there had to be a chapter on my visit to a legal house of prostitution. Later, many counties in Nevada also legalized prostitution, but in the early 1970s, there weren't a lot of choices.

And by the way, Wells, Nevada is way off the beaten path.

My adventures continued, and I spent most of the night at the blackjack tables in Wendover. There is no doubt I was seriously impaired when I returned to the motel. And hardly a surprise that I overslept my wakeup call and the bus to the Salt Flats some miles away.

No one at the motel knew how to get to the Flats, or had any suggestions. I asked about busses back to Salt Lake, and learned Greyhound would be through on Wednesday, three days later

Finally, figuring I had blown it big time, I grabbed my suitcase and went out to the highway and stuck out my thumb. After an hour or so, some guy in a small sports car pulled over and agreed to take me to the Salt Lake airport some 90 miles away. I had no way of connecting with the charter group – no cell phones in those days – so I got out at the airport and went into the United Airlines Counter.

They had only one seat available on a flight to LAX, but it was first class. I pulled out my credit card and gulped down the $90 fare. The flight home was great and the next day, I called Houlgate and told him about my adventure. Somehow, he managed to get STP to reimburse my air fare. I wound up flying first class and got home before the chartered airplane.

Lucky me, in those days.

I was also able to parlay this trip into a project for one of the few science classes I was taking at El Camino College. The class was geography, and when I told the professor about the trip, she agreed I could write my term paper on the Salt Flats.

I borrowed a camera from the Breeze photo department, and was able to go up in a small plane that was hired by the promoters. I shot all manner of pictures for my term paper, not the newspaper, and wrote about the oddities that created this unusual place. I got an A for those efforts, although I'm not sure I'd grade myself that high on missing the bus to the event and back to the airport.

SPORTS IS MY LIFE (OR SO I THOUGHT) (1970S TO 1998)

If you'd have asked me, at any time during my 27½ years at *The Daily Breeze*, I'd have said this was my career and I was not going anywhere.

There were occasional conversations with other papers about positions, but none was ever serious enough to warrant an interview. One was a chance to move to Seattle to cover the Seahawks. Another was a job with the Salt Lake City *Deseret News,* covering winter sports for two years leading up to the 1996 Olympics in that city.

Mostly, I was happy with what I was doing and where I was doing it.

And here's why: Although I started at the Breeze as a desk editor, covering only boxing and auto racing, I quickly started adding assignments that were fun and rewarding.

In 1973, I was assigned to cover the Angels, my first shot at Major League Baseball. A year later, primarily because of logistics and an energy crisis, I was switched to the Dodgers for two years. It was back to the Angels for 1976, then back to the Dodgers in 1977 and 1978. You can look it up, but the Dodgers made the World Series in three of those four years, losing all three.

I was also making a mark among my peers. The Baseball Writers Association of America was still in charge of the sport's press boxes, and had some sway with who was credentialled.

I was soon a vice president of the local chapter, and became president in 1977, serving two terms. That involved staging our annual charity dinner with the teams – an event that often drew 800 or more to a hotel ballroom – and being on stage in a tuxedo after introducing the MC.

Those banquets were held at major hotel ballrooms, such as the Bonaventure in downtown L.A. We attracted talent that was usually on the rise, with our featured comedian one year an unknown named David Letterman.

By my second year, I knew what the "asks" were in the hotel banquet business, and I was given a two-bedroom suite for the duration of the banquet. I hosted players of both teams in the time after their Sunday exhibition game and before the banquet. My date Flossie, and four of our teacher friends, were hosts and also took care of putting out the party favors in the banquet hall.

Those were heady days for a guy in his late 20s.

I later served a number of years as a vice president or president of NASJA, the ski writers' organization.

My trip through the sports world at the Breeze, beginning in the 1970s, covered a lot of ground.

- UCLA football with Pepper Rodgers as coach and a young quarterback named Mark Harmon.
- UCLA and USC basketball as an extra writer, covering the lesser of the two games.
- Kings hockey for two seasons, 1974-75 and 75-76, when they were not very good and played at the Forum.
- Rams football, starting with one trip in 1975 and from 1976-81, including one Super Bowl.
- Raiders football, from 1982 through 1994, when they moved back to Oakland, including one Super Bowl.
- A total of 19 Super Bowl games, including 17 in a row.
- An occasional NBA playoffs game as an extra, or sidebar, writer.
- Horse racing's inaugural Breeders Cup, and at least one additional rendition.

- Three trips to the Indianapolis 500, and a number of other major auto races in California at Riverside and Ontario speedways; and a trip to Las Vegas for the Mint 400 desert off-road race.
- A couple of yacht races along the California course, and stories about sailors in advance of the major TransPac race.
- The 1984 Olympics, exclusively boxing.

While baseball was my lifelong love, and my first major beat at *The Daily Breeze,* football quickly overtook it as my major ongoing professional love affair.

Baseball was the best training ground for a young writer, and I still believe this remains true: You write every day and you write mostly on deadline. You summarize a lot of facts and events into a readable format in a hurry.

And you do it again the next day, and every day for most of six months.

You build relationships with players and coaches, and you are around them on a daily basis. If you write something negative about a player, you need to show up the next day to let him take his shots at you, if he thinks it was not appropriate. If you let the facts tell the story, you rarely have a problem.

Football is a better sport from a lifestyle point of view because they only play one game a week. Granted, it's the most complex game to write about, and if you are doing a Monday Night Game in the East, it's the worst deadline write.

But the rest of the week, you can chase stories, write features, develop angles, and do a more leisurely style of reporting.

The Rams and Raiders made a lot of appearances on Monday Night Football when I was covering them, mostly because they were consistent winners.

In 1980, the Rams were scheduled for a Monday Night game at New Orleans in November. And in an era when boxing was still big time, the Roberto Duran-Sugar Ray Leonard rematch was scheduled for Tuesday night at the same Superdome. Every paper in L.A. wanted their writers to stay over an extra night and cover the fight.

This was Steve Rosenbloom's second year as General Manager of the Saints, so the potential for a big weekend was there before the addition of the fight. In fact, several of us brought girlfriends, who knew Steve and Renee. Patt Robinson was with me, and to make sure we enjoyed it all, we went early, flying on Thursday.

New Orleans is the capital of drinking and fine dining, so we had worked our way through four nights of stressful living before game time on Monday night. Fortunately, the Rams won an easy game. Then came a long day Tuesday before the fight, and finally a flight home on Wednesday. Six nights in New Orleans can challenge anyone.

I did not miss baseball when I shifted fulltime to football, but when football was taken away from Southern California in 1995, I missed it dearly. The departure of the Rams for St. Louis and the Raiders back to Oakland hastened my move to a second career in education.

The one thing I learned over and over again, you can't count on anything being permanent.

ON THE ROAD: BAKERSFIELD (1973)

I was always looking for something different to write about and was always pitching ideas to Sports Editor Mike Waldner. My batting average wasn't very good, but every once in a while, I'd come up with something that was novel enough, cheap enough, and might make a good story or two.

In 1973, I was on my first year covering baseball, with the Angels, and loving it. But the *Daily Breeze* almost never traveled with the Angels (only the Dodgers) and so my assignment was home games only.

This was before the movie, "Bull Durham," and at a time when minor league baseball was still mysterious and intriguing. I pitched this idea: Let me go to Bakersfield, home of the single-A Bakersfield Dodgers, and cover a few home games and then take a road trip with them. Find out what life was like in the low minors, write about a couple of prospects from the South Bay, and get away from home.

Perhaps because I would be driving, staying in the hotels where the teams stayed (Best Westerns) and trying to live on minor-league meal money, it was cheap enough to have a chance.

Let me explain meal money: Major League players that year received $28 in meal money for every day on the road. When the Dodgers got on their plane for a 10-day road trip, each of them received an envelope with $280 in cash. Flash forward to recent years and the figure is $105 per day. Meal money has always been major league for the players at the top.

But in 1973, when I went on the road with the Bakersfield Dodgers, the meal money for Class-A teams was $7.50 per day. Even then, that works out to an Egg McMuffin, a Big Mac and some fries. Most of the players tried to make it work by stuffing down a couple of free ball park hot dogs after the game.

Major league baseball was 20 years away from the realization that nutrition mattered. They were still living in the Babe Ruth Era of six hot dogs and six beers makes for a home run hitter.

I managed to make the $7.50 a day work, like the players, by eating ball park food. But then I wound up in the bar at night, and my Scotch habit was a budget-buster.

The California League was a major stop for future major leaguers in those days – and remained so until the 2020 Pandemic threatened to crush minor-league baseball.

Players were often in their second stop as a professional by the time they got to Bakersfield, in the Dodger system. Or Modesto, in the St. Louis Cardinals' minor-league hierarchy. Most were kids drafted out of high school, so they might have been 19 or 20 years old.

Typically, they'd left high school for a short-season stint in Rookie Ball the year before, and were now becoming full-fledged minor leaguers. Some were true prospects with the eye of the big club on them. But the pyramid of minor league baseball in 1973 was as challenging as ever. Many started rookie ball and made it to Class A, fewer progressed to double-A, then triple-A, and even fewer ever played in the majors.

When I got to Bakersfield in July 1973, it was 100 degrees at 3 o'clock in the afternoon, and likely to get hotter before the sun set.

Players lived for free in rooms donated by community families, but were required to be at the ballpark at least four hours before game time.

For that adventure, I agreed to arrive for the last game of a homestand, then get up early the next day to catch an 8 a.m. bus up the central valley to Modesto. The Dodgers would play three games against the Redbirds, then bus home after the last game.

I would return to finish up with a couple of more games at Bakersfield before returning to the South Bay.

While I was only 25 at the time, I felt considerably older than the young players, having spent two years overseas in the Navy, plus having been a working professional for several years. Aside from baseball, most of us had little to talk about.

But there was one player – and I'm at a loss for his name, which confirms that he did not climb to the top of the pyramid – who gravitated towards me and initiated a conversation. He was a pitcher, maybe 22 or 23, who was making a second run through single-A ball after moving up to double-A a couple of years earlier before blowing out his pitching arm. He had gotten to spring training with the major-league team, and had a much higher quality uniform than the hand-me-downs the other players wore. His actually had his name on the back.

On one of the interminable days of sitting around the motel in Modesto, he wound up in my room, and sipped a couple of beers while we watched the All-Star Game. He seemed worldly compared to his teammates. No Crash Davis, mind you, but the Bull Durham analogy fits. He had been around minor-league baseball for at least four seasons, which was a lifetime.

When we got to Modesto, I spent a little time with Redbirds manager Bobby Dews, a minor-league lifer who helped provide me with a notebook full of anecdotes and perspective. He was 20 years into his journey around the minor leagues, with his second or third organization, and lived for the job that didn't pay him enough to give up his offseason job.

A few years later, Dews wound up with the Braves, and made to the majors as a coach. He wound up staying long enough as a major-league coach to earn a pension. But when I met him, he was slogging through the low minors, earning $1,000 or $1,500 a month, and happy to let a visiting writer buy him a few cocktails after a game.

The results of the games on that trip are long lost in the memory bank, but I remember a few of the events:

- After the first game in Modesto, Dews was so unhappy with his players' effort that he kept them for a post-game practice. It was 10 o'clock at night, and he told the players to send their girlfriends home. They stayed on the field for 45 minutes or so of basic training after a mid-season game.
- The amenities that major-league players take for granted are missing in the low minors. Players didn't have to launder their own

uniforms, but they did have to launder the long white, sanitary socks if they went through more than one pair a game, which most did.

- Players from all over the country wind up playing minor-league ball in the California League, but after a season of playing up and down the Golden State, they all wind up with southern accents. Maybe it's because many of the coaches toiled for teams in the south early in their careers. Come to think of it, a large portion of sailors leave the Navy with a southern accent, too.

- Minor league baseball always thrived on promotions. One night in Modesto, they trotted out a sign with a hole about the size of a manhole cover and brought three people from the stands to the field to try hitting the target with a baseball. Get the ball through the hole from 60 feet away, and win $100. By some incredible stroke of luck, I was chosen to participate – not calling it luck, since the P.R. man did the choosing. Perhaps confirming why I was not on the field, or playing ball at any level, I was 0-for-3 on my tries.

- There are no major success stories from those I met and wrote about that summer in Bakersfield. I can't remember the name of a single player who advanced to the majors from either the Dodgers or the Redbirds. But I did enjoy seeing Bobby Dews when he was traveling with the Braves years later and they would play the Dodgers.

Minor league baseball was a fascination for me starting when I fell in love with the sport when I was 8 or 10 years old. In those days, you could follow every team in every league through the weekly pages of *The Sporting News*. They ran boxscores of every team – albeit a week or 10 days behind – so you could follow all of the players.

One of my favorites in the late 1950s was a Dodger second baseman at the double-A level named …. Bobby Cox. Twenty plus years later, he was managing in the major leagues, and he and I were staying at the same hotel for the World Series. I got a lot of his phone calls that year. Oh, and Bobby Dews was on his coaching staff at Atlanta.

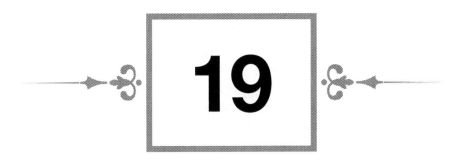

THREE BIG EVENTS (1974)

So many things shape our lives, but few can match the three events that occurred in Fall 1974 for their impact on my decision to re-invent myself with some major changes.

The three events, in order:

- My mother, Lorena Bernell (Walker) Cox, died in September.
- My wife, Lorraine Marise (Quinn) Cox, files papers for divorce after about 5½ years of marriage.
- My father, Kenneth William Cox, died in late December.

Each was an important event on its own merits. Together, they pretty much taught me that there was no time like the present to do a little reshaping.

For starters, my parents had spent their entire lives "saving for a vacation," or a car, or a trip, or a house. But something always got in the way, hence they never did any of the things they dreamed about. Part of that was lousy money management, being trapped in the lower strata of the economy. But part of it also was the treadmill approach.

As for the marriage to Lorraine, the inevitability of that divorce comes to mind. We got married for all the wrong reasons, we each wanted something different from the marriage, and frankly, I wasn't all that committed to the concept from the beginning.

My mother's death came as a surprise, only in the fact that my parents never shared important information with their children. I knew she had had double mastectomy surgery in the late 1950s, before we went to Idaho, so cancer was a major presence in her life. But parents and kids of that era did not have the open and free-flowing exchange of information that we now take for granted.

I just learned from my dad that she was in the hospital, and I should come visit. Soon. My grandmother, Mimmie, did a better job of explaining the situation to me than my father had. She told me that Rena, her daughter, was very sick and probably wasn't going to make it.

A day or so later, after I visited her and found her incredibly drugged up and feeling no pain, she passed away. At least the doctors eased her final days. To this day, I don't know the type of cancer, or how it went undetected until the bitter end. The fact my parents were the working poor and had no health insurance suggested no regular doctor visits.

Maybe she was masking her pain with the six-pack of Brew 102 beer that she and my father each consumed nightly.

After she passed, I reminded my father and brother that she did not want a burial we could not afford, and had agreed to cremation. Her brother Clyde and his family, who were active in the Presbyterian church, arranged for a memorial service one afternoon.

A few weeks later, the pieces started to fall apart for my father. Since he and his wife were the traditional couple who managed apartment buildings in those days, they lived rent-free. She collected the rents, found new tenants, and handled the office chores. He took care of the minor maintenance. A month or two after Mom's death, the owner told Dad he would be looking for a new couple to manage the apartment building.

Nothing had been settled by early December and there was at least one conversation about my father and me renting an apartment together, since I was now on my own as well.

But before that possibility could come into play, Dad was taking care of one of those little managerial chores. He was standing on a ladder, changing one of the light bulbs in the common area of the building, when he fell and landed on his head. Santa Monica Hospital kept him alive for another 10 days or so, but he never spoke another word. And one night, an attending doctor told me about some of the options. This was before a number of major court cases about end-of-life issues, so my giving him a verbal consent was enough. Next time extraordinary issues were required to save Kenny Cox, they were not used, per the wishes of the family (me).

Another cremation, no memorial service this time. And another life-changing event for me. Handling my parents' affairs, I became the executor of the estate, along with an attorney friend. Estate is a legal term, not particularly descriptive. There was a $5,000 life insurance policy through his work. And since his daughter from a previous marriage was still alive, that was split three ways. Some estate.

In between these events, Lorraine and I finally consummated the dissipation of our marriage. While I was not particularly good about keeping the marriage vows, the end came on a phone call from a girl I had met in a bar – and nothing had happened. But the late-night phone call, answered by Lorraine, pretty much gave her the justification she had been seeking.

A day or two later, she moved back to Glendale and the family compound.

At the age of 27, both my parents had died, and my wife filed for divorce.

That gave me a lot of time for reflection and triggered a period of time that might be loosely called my Mickey Mantle Stage. Like the baseball great, I decided I was not going to live a long life – I had it in the back of my mind that 42 was about it – and unlike my folks, I wasn't going to spend my time saving to do something.

Did anyone say credit? I embraced the feeling that money was not going to come between me and a good time.

I also learned from my new friends about a sport that would shape my life, skiing. I had been playing beach volleyball that summer with a group of teachers, and they talked a lot about skiing as the summer was winding down.

First came attending ski club meetings. These were the best singles hangouts I'd ever experienced. And this was before I ever strapped on a ski.

Two nights a month, singles in the Beach Cities Ski Club would meet at a restaurant in Manhattan Beach. On two other nights, South Bay Ski Club would meet. That was four nights to meet a ton of young (and not-so-young) women in a setting conducive to getting to know one another.

I was hooked on skiing before I ever went skiing. It was a lifestyle easy to embrace in 1974.

On the day after Christmas, 1974, a friend and I drove to Mammoth. I rented skis and took lessons, hoping to be good enough in three days to ski with my girlfriend at the time.

Lesson No. 1: Listen to the ski instructor. In the adult group lessons of those days, the idea was to get some sort of skill imparted in the 4-hour session. Because I fancied myself an athlete, and thought my mostly female classmates were moving kind of slow, I tried to do more than was being asked. And probably didn't listen very well. I'm sure I fell 100 times and tired myself out so much that I was dozing off on the bar at the Yodeler Inn across from the main lodge at Mammoth.

But I listened better the next day, and the next. And by the fourth day, I was able to keep up with the intermediate skiing group that included my girlfriend.

I was driven to become a competent skier, and obsessively pursued that goal in the weeks, months and years to come.

Skiing quickly became my major non-working activity. I skied more than 25 days that first season. I got into a group that rented a condo for the season, I bought skis, boots and clothes, and I started shaping my life around ski trips.

I also joined the Southern California Ski Writers, a group that provided access to ski areas and ski area marketing types, and opening the door to free lift tickets. By my second year, I had bought a season pass to Mammoth Mountain for $300 (which was pegged at 30 days use at the rate of $10 a day). A month or two later, on a Ski Writers trip to Mammoth, the marketing director refunded the price of my ticket and I was skiing free.

That has continued to this day. I had a complimentary season pass at Mammoth for in excess of 30 years, including privileges for wife and kids. I was writing a weekly column about things skiing, and the access provided by Mammoth and other ski areas resulted in a lot of fun columns.

While writing about skiing is a little different that writing about football or baseball – no winners and losers every day – it was a great diversion for me. I wrote about the resorts, the equipment, the people, the innovations, the competitions, the reasons for enjoying the sport, and just about anything that might be of interest to the skiing public.

Typically, newspapers ran a skiing column, but since nobody on the staff was a skier, they didn't care much what you wrote about, as long as it was there on time and in a usable format. For more than 20 years, my column was syndicated to the other Copley Newspapers.

I also started repackaging and selling many of the pieces to other newspapers. Destination pieces were snapped up by newspaper travel sections. Similar to sports sections and the weekly skiing column, they just needed to fill an annual Ski Travel Advertising section. If some writer in L.A. had offered us a piece on visiting Banff, or Colorado, and he had pictures, that made the section. There were a lot of checks for $50 or $100 in those days for the free-lance ski writing business. It was also a good thing from an income tax perspective, since I was writing off a lot of the expenses, and the ski resorts were comping the rest.

One of the best received pieces I ever did was on helicopter skiing out of Whistler, B.C., and that produced a cover story for *Newsday*, the giant paper on Long Island, N.Y. Part of the reason was a part-time heli-guide and aspiring photographer, who took some great pictures, and one became the full-page color cover of the Travel Section. I think I got $500 for that story/picture combination, which I split with the photographer.

There was an annual competition for best ski story and best ski column, run by the national ski writers association, which became NASJA (North American Snowsports Journalists Association) and I went on a streak where I dominated the annual competitions. I remain the single all-time winner with seven best story awards. Each of which produced a free trip to the annual meeting, and often a pair of skis or a quality parka from a big-name sponsor.

I got involved in NASJA, and spent nearly 20 years scouting locations for and convincing resorts to host the annual journalists' convention.

For about 15 years, I was vice president of meetings and travel for NASJA, and brought our large spring event to ski areas in Canada, most of the Rocky Mountain states, and even once each to the northeast and Midwest. I loved putting on our annual meeting, from the initial conversations that sparked the bidding process through to the final gala event each year.

It helped that I was winning writing awards most years and able to bring Nancy and sometimes the kids for free or at reduced rates.

After stalling as long as I could, I finally moved up to President of NASJA and served in that capacity for two terms, or four years. I continued on the board for another four years as past president. NASJA was a once thriving group that had nationwide representation and could bring 150 to 200 people to a ski area for the annual convention in March or April.

But like the newspaper industry, ski writing went into a tumble and our membership declined precipitously. Fewer newspapers meant fewer chances to write and sell ski columns, and in recent years, NASJA's membership had dwindled to perhaps 50 active writers.

There were hundreds of ski columns over the years, maybe even thousands, as I skied my way around almost 100 resorts and enjoyed writing about them. Virtually everything I did as a skier was a column, from visiting resorts to having boots custom fitted to learning the latest instructional techniques. In short, all of skiing was my beat and I loved producing the weekly columns.

Of those thousands of columns, only one is framed and displayed in my den.

In spring 1995, young son Randy made his first trip out of children's ski school for a run on the beginning slopes with his parents. He was four years old, and while we were avid skiers, we could only hope that would be the case with him. When we found the column recently, Randy laminated it for me and it hangs in the den. He went on to become a professional ski instructor and spent several years in the industry at two different resorts.

As he grew into his teens, and became a strong skier after a brief venture into snowboarding, he was able to accompany me on trips to many resorts to set up NASJA events.

In particular, we had a great trip to Crested Butte in advance of one of our best-ever conventions. During our time there, he and I skied with a couple who were part-time instructors, and he got to see how the locals skied the mountain.

And one night at dinner at a pizza joint, we were joined by former racer and free skiing star Kim Reichhelm, who was a rock star in her 30s in those days. When she suggested he and she try an innovative pizza with potatoes and something else, he suddenly became an adventurous eater.

When you are 16 years old and a knockout superstar skier in her 30s is paying attention to you, life is pretty good

When Randy was 19, he and I went on a big adventure to Whistler Mountain, in British Columbia, and experienced the inevitable transition that happens in every skiing family.

There is only one day when a father and son are exactly equal in ski ability – it's the day before the son moves ahead and becomes the dominant skier.

As Randy moved into his 20s, and became a professional ski instructor, he helped me coordinate several of the annual NASJA events.

At NASJA's 50th annual meeting at Mammoth in 2013, I was leading a group of ski area marketing types on a tour off the top at Mammoth, and when the high winds made it tough to get off the front. I had committed, but Randy wisely took the five women off the back and got them down in the best possible manner.

Allie and I did not get as much time on the slopes as Randy and I, primarily because of her commitments to softball and volleyball, which would help pave her way to college. But her athleticism and competitive juices meant she would move swiftly to the point of becoming a strong skier.

One day during her college years, she and I were at Mammoth for a short trip, and came across a timed race course. She wanted to have a go of it, and since I'd spent 20 years working on ski racing skills, I was game. What I wasn't prepared for was her beating me. Not once, but twice.

Same story about a father and daughter and their skiing abilities, it seems. In her case, athletic abilities trumped many days of lessons and practice.

MAMMOTH: SEMI-LOCAL
(1974 TO PRESENT)

I fell in love with Mammoth, and skiing, almost at first sight. On Dec. 26, 1974, near the end of that year when so much of my life changed, I drove to Mammoth in my basic 1972 Toyota Corolla with friend Ted Andrini.

He was part of the group of teachers I had started to hang out with at the beach that summer, and was going to be my first guide to Mammoth and skiing. On the drive up, I would ask questions, because this was an adventure of the first order. I knew nothing about skiing, or Mammoth, except that a lot of people I had come to like and admire were hooked.

My first skiing lesson on Dec. 27 – the holidays meant monster crowd days then, as now – was a humbling experience.

By the second day's lesson I was listening better, and by my third day on skis, I was able to tag along with the group of intermediate skiers that included my girlfriend. And I was hooked. Skiing was outdoors, physical, social, and involved a lot of chances to stop for a drink. What's not to like?

That first winter, I was part of a group of guys that rented a small condo and paid $5 or $6 a night to sleep there. By the end of the second winter, I had progressed to fairly decent as a skier, had acquired the appropriate clothing and equipment, and realized this was my lifestyle.

At the end of the second ski season, 1975-76, I put together a group with Andrini and Flossie Duff and we purchased a new condo for $36,900.

More importantly, the monthly payments were $232.52 and this condo was big enough to rent out bed space for $10 a night. And we were making our payments.

A little lesson in economics: Each of us put in a total of $3,333, for a starting fund of $10k, which covered down payment, closing costs, and enough to furnish the condo through garage sales. On July 4th weekend, we rented a U-Haul truck and furnished our place at St. Moritz Villas (No. 31).

Ted drifted away from skiing, and after a couple of years, Flossie and I broke up. She moved to Mammoth with her boyfriend who had finally left his wife. And I had a great condo. I was there constantly, rented out beds, and started crafting a lifestyle.

Flash forward about eight years, and Flossie and Ted wanted to pull out. A couple of real estate savvy friends helped me put together a deal that took advantage of the rising market. We re-financed and each of the two initial partners got $30,000 – nearly ten times their initial investment – and I took on three new partners. But we also had a payment of nearly $1,000 a month.

There was also a real estate adventure in which I put together a small group to buy a trailer home in a nearby park, and was doing the same renting that out. But two of the partners had a pack of kids, and were bringing them every weekend, which killed the market for my singles friends. I got out of that quickly.

But real estate is only a small part of the Mammoth adventure.

The mountain, which I came to love and embrace in every way, became my home away from home. The Village, and later the Town after incorporation, was a place that was my refuge from the world.

I crafted a lifestyle that worked something like this: Because I worked more than 5 days a week, counting travel, playoffs games, Super Bowls, and other requirements, during the football season, I received about 10 days of comp time in an unofficial deal with Sports Editor Mike Waldner.

Those 10 days, plus my three weeks of vacation, added up to a pile of days.

I rarely got to Mammoth until after the Super Bowl, but when football season ended, my Mammoth time began. Usually I would fly home from wherever the Super Bowl was on Monday, do laundry, pay bills and pack on Tuesday, and be en route to Mammoth on Wednesday. Often, I would stay for 10 days or two weeks to start the season and get into skiing shape.

Then I would start a routine that I could often stretch until early April: Work Monday and Tuesday on the morning sports copy desk, then drive to Mammoth, and stay five days. I would come home after racing on Sunday, then repeat the process the next week.

I was doing five days a week in Mammoth and two days at home. With modest variations, this went on for most of 20 years.

One of my friends in Mammoth, author Robert Blair Kaiser, took to calling me the "semi-local" when introducing me to friends. In those days, the highest compliment was to be a local in Mammoth. That put you above the crowd of weekenders who surged into town every Friday night and left every Sunday night.

Skiing was the reason for being in Mammoth and – as I was able to write in several free-lance magazine articles – the badge of honor. Sure, you could drive an expensive car, and you could buy the most fashionable and pricey ski clothing, but could you turn the skis? Were you the king of the intermediate slopes around Warming Hut 2, or did you spend your time on "the top?"

I learned early on that nobody serious about skiing was going to listen if you were talking about your exploits on runs named Blue Bird, or Hansel and Gretel. If you were talking about a run off The Top, be it a successful run or even a monstrous crash, people listened. In short, if you were a serious skier, people were interested in your stories.

That was my goal and I went at it with the same passion and drive that I pursued everything else in life. I needed to be a strong enough skier that I could pretty much go anywhere, in any conditions, and ski with anybody on the mountain. I was skiing at least five days a week, 10 plus weeks a year, and more than 50 days a season, with that goal in mind.

And with the exception of the handful of runs off the top that are treated with reverence by the 100 or so great skiers who can manage them, I succeeded. *Huevos Grande* does not mean Big Eggs, but something close, and if you could not make three perfect turns in an elevator shaft, then jump a big flippin' rock, and land another perfect turn, your eggs weren't big enough to be there.

But I was nearly everywhere else on the top. I raced on the weekends, sometimes with success, and I skied with the top skiers in the Race Department and Ski School. Many of these skiers were my friends from the bars at night, which was part of the reason Mammoth was so perfect for me.

It didn't matter how impaired you got at night, if you could face the cold, crisp morning air, and get back out there on your skis. Mammoth respected skiers, and later snowboarders. A lot more than it respected your Mercedes, or your American Express Black Card.

I made a few lasting friends in Mammoth. John Armstrong was initially a race coach, then became head of the department, and later was in charge of all ski instruction. He also served terms as president of the U.S. Ski Coaches Association and the Professional Ski Instructors of America, in addition to coaching with the U.S. Ski Team.

He had a great sense of humor, could weave a speech from Rudyard Kipling to the Rolling Stones to ski instruction, and was fun to be around as well as to talk skiing with. He was my resource for many ski columns and was always available to share his knowledge.

When I became vice president of NASJA (the ski journalists organization) and was putting on an annual meeting in Banff, I was able to get John to come along as our guest speaker at the gala banquet. We also worked together when Mammoth hosted NASJA, and on a variety of other projects.

One year I was able to get him a pair of tickets for the Super Bowl in San Francisco, and he brought along a ski instructor friend and bon vivant named Scottie Bartholomew.

Asked how he had selected Scottie, he said, "Well, for a skiing trip, you pick the best skier. And for a trip to the party that is the Super Bowl, you pick the best partier. That would be Scottie."

Mammoth was so much a home for me, I always had a home bar, the place where I could be found on a nightly basis. At one time, it was the Cask and Cleaver, because they built up a happy hour business by offering two-for-one drinks and free hors d'oeuvres.

One year, during the Steve Rosenbloom vs. Georgia (Rosenbloom) Frontiere spat, I broke a story about the owner of the Rams crying in her private suite because she was getting booed. The Sports Talk radio show wanted to interview me, and tracked me down at the Cask and Cleaver – again, no cell phones. We quickly realized the bar was a lousy background for a radio interview, so I drove home and did the interview from my condo.

After the Cask stopped offering 2-for-1 drinks, I wound up drifting to another bar favored by the local crowd, Josh Slocum's on Main Street. This is where I knew I could find a friend, no matter the day of the week or whether I had just gotten back from a Super Bowl in New Orleans or been away for only a day or two.

The late 1970s and early 1980s were a great time to be in Mammoth. That was when it was said, "there's more snow in town than on the mountain." But they weren't talking about the 12 feet of powder outside the Main Lodge.

Mammoth was a center of experimentation with cocaine at a time when it was popular in all levels of society. I'm not sure you could actually buy it across the bar in most places, but you certainly could find someone who would meet you outside or in the men's room to transact a business deal.

As society realized what a bad idea this drug was, it became less of a factor in Mammoth. Of course, we were all growing up a little, too. The experiments of our 20s and early 30s seemed less and less intelligent as we started to sneak up on maturity.

One year when I had just returned from a Super Bowl and had driven to Mammoth I was still learning some of these lessons. I had rented out my condo, so was staying in a room the ski area comped me at the Mammoth Mountain Inn.

I arrived in town after a cross-country flight, at a town where the elevation was 8,000 feet, then up to the mountain, where it was 9,000 feet. I had also stopped at Slocum's for one (or maybe 10) cocktails, and may have dabbled in a little of the powder.

The next morning, after drinking coffee at breakfast, I suddenly felt my heart pounding, like it was trying to jump out of my chest. I laid on the bench by my locker for a few moments and when it did not stop, went to the Ski Patrol First Aid station. Apparently, I was not doing well, because they started doing a series of tests. I asked them to call up to the Race Department and get my friend John Armstrong.

He came down and rode in the ambulance with me when it was time to head to the hospital. In a few moments in the emergency room, they immediately diagnosed *tachycardia* (racing of the heart, basically) and resolved the problem. I was kept in the hospital for a day to make sure. That afternoon and evening, I had about 20 visitors.

One nurse, after looking at my chart and then noting the crowd in my room, said, "For a guy who just got into town last night, you sure made a lot of friends in a hurry."

Rumors spread among the ski club crowd that I had sustained a massive heart attack, or worse. When I showed up for the races on the weekend, it was a major surprise. When I beat my friend Mike Fiore in our race – and he was notorious as a bad loser – I taunted him: "You just lost to a guy who was in the emergency room a couple of days ago." And he threw a ski pole and skied off.

I later learned that tachycardia can be caused by a variety of factors, including altitude, booze, drugs, caffeine, lack of sleep and a few others. I was able to tell the paramedic to check "all of the above" in my case.

I later wrote a column about it – everything I did in skiing or Mammoth usually found its way into a column. I may have been a little vague about the contributing factors. But it was an adventure I felt needed to be written about.

One adventure that did not make a column would have been titled AKA McKay.

In the midst of one winter in the early 1980s, a 30ish woman showed up in Mammoth, and got a job working as a clerk in the Race Department office. She eventually wound up moving into my condo as a tenant, which was convenient for her and me. She had a gift of gab and a way of charming people. When I fancied a new pair of Rossignol skis, she found a way to wangle a pair from the ski company rep, who was in town for a race. She was the life of the party, and we often had a lot of parties at the condo.

She went by the name Judy McKay. She often hung out with a couple of the lesbians who worked in the Race Department, but she may also have been open to other options.

Toward the end of the winter, she acquired a big black Lab, a dog which overpowered the condo. One day when I was down south, she called to say the dog "had eaten" my sofa. When I asked if she meant he chewed a little on the leg, she said, "no, he ate it." She found a way to replace that sofa with a new one on credit from a store in Bishop. Like I said, Judy had a way with people.

When the season ended, and she was laid off by the mountain, I assumed she had just packed up and moved on. We had never much talked about her background, or her future. Mammoth was like that. You were just there.

A couple of months later, I got a call from a detective with the Mono County Sheriffs, who wanted to ask me some questions about Judy AKA McKay. I immediate asked about the AKA – also known as – and learned Judy went by several names.

She arrived in Mammoth that February, having just been paroled from one of California's women's prisons. And the reason they were investigating her, was that the Race Department's end-of-season audit came up thousands of dollars short. Ski racing was very much a cash business in those days. Ten bucks to enter a race, twenty bucks for a race clinic. Apparently, Judy was funneling a lot of those tens and twenties away from the cash drawer.

Later, Race Department Chief Dennis Agee called me and wanted to blame me for Judy. I reminded him that he'd hired her and I only met her after he put her to work. Sure, I rented a bed to her for a couple of months, but she was stealing money from his office.

Neither Agee nor I was able to help the detective much, and the legend of Judy AKA McKay simmered for a while. Eventually, she was arrested for some kind of money scam in a mining town elsewhere in the High Sierra. Seems that McKay, or whatever her real name was, had been in jail for similar adventures and had just gotten back to her roots. Mammoth being a very easy-going place in those days, she was hired and handling cash without so much as a background check.

I wound up with new skis in exchange for the room she used, and a new couch for the one her dog had eaten. And the Race Department and I had a story to share for years to come. Rumor has it AKA McKay spent a few months in jail, then moved on to another town.

That St. Moritz condo was eventually lost due to a combination of factors. When we refinanced and quadrupled the monthly payment, it was with the knowledge that two of our new partners were financially solid.

John Funtsch and I were scrambling month to month in the '70s, but Kris Cox and Gary Foster were business owners.

Then came a real estate crash. Mammoth's market took a dive when the U.S. Geological Survey came out with a definitive study that Mammoth's volcano would surely erupt sometime in the next 1,000 years. This made news. And the TV stations in L.A. were showing footage of Kilauea erupting in Hawaii every night, then tagging on the story that "meanwhile in Mammoth, the USGS is predicting a volcanic eruption sometime in the next 1,000 years."

Nobody heard 1,000 years. Suddenly the image was of people skiing on flowing lava at Mammoth. The town and county joined the panic mode and built a road out of town called the "scenic route" which was widely and derisively known as the Escape Route.

And Mammoth real estate plunged. Then two of my partners moved away and left John and I with a $1,000 monthly nut we could not cover by renting beds for $10 a night. The property went into foreclosure and was gone after 10 great years. And I became a guest, or renter, in other people's homes.

While Ted and Flossie cashed out a couple of years earlier for $30K each, I had 50 percent of nothing.

Mammoth was still home; it was just not quite as cozy.

Later, when we were raising young kids, I was able to connect through a local friend, and get half-price lodging for three couples. Often it was the Catozzis or the Benzes and us, although another couple may have been part of some of those trips. We'd rent a four-bedroom condo for four nights, and live the life of young parents in the mountains.

One year I put together a deal where niece Toriann would cut a couple of days of school and come with us as a babysitter for the three families for the 4-day weekend. We'd give her a heathy amount of money and she gave us the peace of mind to enjoy our skiing adventure.

My parents, Ken and Rena Cox (1947)

Me in an early picture, circa 1953

Me and Ronnie as Cub Scouts (1957)

Ronnie and me in our baseball uniforms (1957)

Me in a school picture (1957)

Me with the flat-top cut of the era (1961)

My first column mug shot at the Citizen-News (1965)

Our family at Ronnie's wedding (1967)

Navy Seaman Cox at the Defense Information School (1968)

Me and Lorraine were married in Las Vegas (1969)

Captain Ray Hawkins honored my service at NAS Atsugi, Japan.
He previously led the Blue Angels shown in picture (1970)

Ski racing was a major part of my life at Mammoth Mountain (1983)

Nancy and I were married on a beautiful day at Palos Verdes (1987)

Teachers get their school pictures every year (2001)

Lisa was at the Forum when I received my Master's
Degree in Educational Administration (2002)

Randy (No. 78) playing right tackle for Torrance High's football team (2008)

Nancy and I saluted Randy on Senior Night (2008)

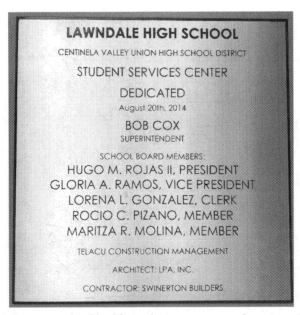

LAWNDALE HIGH SCHOOL

CENTINELA VALLEY UNION HIGH SCHOOL DISTRICT

STUDENT SERVICES CENTER

DEDICATED

August 20th, 2014

BOB COX
SUPERINTENDENT

SCHOOL BOARD MEMBERS:

HUGO M. ROJAS II, PRESIDENT
GLORIA A. RAMOS, VICE PRESIDENT
LORENA L. GONZALEZ, CLERK
ROCIO C. PIZANO, MEMBER
MARITZA R. MOLINA, MEMBER

TELACU CONSTRUCTION MANAGEMENT

ARCHITECT: LPA, INC.

CONTRACTOR: SWINERTON BUILDERS

We opened three new school buildings during my year as Superintendent (2014)

Allie pitched four years for Wheaton College in Massachusetts, including one year when they went to the NCAA Super Regionals (2015)

We celebrated my retirement with a cruise in the Mediterranean Sea (2015)

Allie, Nancy, Randy, Sylvie and I on the beach on Maui
for Randy and Sylvie's wedding (2017)

Allie receives her white coat as she begins veterinary medicine school (2018)

Our three grand-daughters got together when Geneva Cox
visited Sabrina and Sydney Bulsombut (2020)

Lisa's family (from left), Sabrina, Nat, Sydney and
Lisa gathered for Nat's birthday (2020)

Nancy and I enjoying an annual cruise (2019)

THE SUN ALSO RISES (1976)

I was going through my second Hemingway phase in the mid-1970s, having once again read a couple of his classic novels, possibly for an assignment for a class at El Camino College. It was easy to get hooked on some of Hemingway's books, notably *The Sun Also Rises*, which features the bull fighting scene in Spain between the world wars.

Driving south to Tijuana for the bull fights became a semi-regular part of our routine when I was dating Flossie Duff. Typically, if the Angels were out of town, I would be working the night sports desk on Friday and Saturday nights. We would then take off Sunday morning for the Mexican border town.

Much like so many things we did in the 1970s, things were much different than now. It was not difficult to cross the border at Tijuana – no border walls and surprisingly minimal traffic at the international crossings – and thousands of Americans did it every day.

Bull-fighting was a centerpiece of our trips to Mexico, but we also attended the Jai Alai Fronton a few times, and did some shopping in the city. (It should be noted this was before I adapted the quote, "Women go shopping, and men go buying," as a motto). But shopping in Tijuana was a sporting event from my perspective, since you were competing with the clerk on price for every item you purchased. A little Spanish helped, but you could barter in English, too, and both Flossie and I were very competitive. Sometimes the shopping was as much a game as any other sport.

We would drive down Sunday morning, buy Mexican auto insurance before crossing the border, then check into our hotel and enjoy the shops in the early afternoon. The bull fights began at 4 p.m., at one of two Tijuana bull rings, either downtown or the one "on the beach" or closer to Rosarito Beach.

I realize in the climate when this is being written, bull-fighting might seem controversial for its inhumanity to animals. But in the 1970s, it was thriving and was covered as a sport in the Spanish language newspapers.

Because Papa Hemingway loved it, and because he wrote lovingly of the matadors, the toros and the ceremony of each event, I found it attractive when I was in my 20s. I studied the sport, learned who the rock star matadors were, and who to follow among the rising young ones. We became savvy enough to know when we were watching an artistic performance. This went on for a couple of summers, perhaps 1976 and 1977, before we lost interest.

After the bull fight, especially when it was at the downtown location, there was usually a thriving party at the hotel where the matadors stayed. We often stayed there as well. Much drinking and celebration, especially if the matadors had all survived without serious injury.

A couple of times, we'd the go to the Jai Alai games, which had pari-mutuel betting on the matches. While I loved the sporting aspects of jai alai, and while I would bet on anything in those days, I soured on betting on lowly paid human beings competing. The opportunities for a possible fixed match were too great.

One weekend, Flossie got excited about buying Mexican men's shirts, made out of jeans material, which she would then embroider and send out as gifts. She decided that would be her gift for a number of men on her holiday list, and I think she bargained a great price for perhaps 18 shirts.

We had driven back and forth across the U.S.-Mexico border a dozen times or more, and barely got a smile or a wave from U.S. Border Patrol. But the day we had 18 shirts, something alerted the agents, and we were asked to pull into the inspection area.

Since we were not smuggling drugs, and didn't have more than one bottle of tequila each, we were not worried. Until we were accused of smuggling a forbidden item – the shirts. It seems there was a cotton embargo in place in the 1970s, and we were in violation.

It was explained we could have a few shirts, for personal use, but 18 shirts looked like we were importing them to sell, and that was a violation.

The competitor in Flossie immediately kicked in. She was not going to give up her shirts, although the total value of what we had can't have exceeded $100.

We took the shirts back across the border, into Mexico, and went back to the store where we had bought them and the salesman agreed to hold them for us over night. We re-crossed the border, and drove the three hours north to Redondo Beach, all the while figuring out how to beat the system.

Flossie took the next day off from teaching, and we switched cars and returned south with a plan. We figured my license plate was now marked in the Border Patrol computer, so we went back in her car.

Our plan: We would wrap a dozen of the shirts in individual bags with names on them, as gifts. I would take six of them – the most we figured I could claim as personal use – and bring them across through the walking gate. We spent a lot of time on this plan and were prepared for confrontations on two fronts.

We both had our adrenalin up and were ready to win this battle.

Little need. She cruised through the drive-across border without so much as a nod. And similarly, I walked across with a bag that nobody wanted to inspect.

We won battle of the cotton embargo, and were not incarcerated as smugglers.

RECONNECTING TO FAMILY (1978)

One day in the spring of 1978, I received a telephone call that rattled my cage and ended my self-imposed exile from family members.

I was living with Patt Robinson and her daughter Stacee at the time, and the female voice on the telephone was calling to rip me a new one. It was a voice I had never heard, but she spoke with an authority that surprised me.

"Hey, do you realize your grandmother Mimmie is in Torrance and you have made no attempt to see her?" And before I could respond, she added, "You probably don't remember me, but this is your cousin Jennifer."

After my parents passed away in the last few months of 1974, I was searching for who I was and who should be a part of my life. I was not certain there was a place for extended family. I pretty much excommunicated myself from family members.

I hadn't specifically excluded my grandmother, known forever as Mimmie although her name was Mildred Krause. But she was living in Arizona at the time, so wasn't really on my radar. And my cousin Jennifer? She was a second cousin, oldest daughter of Paula, and last I'd seen or heard from her, she was a little kid.

Yet here she was telling me I'd better find a way to connect with Mimmie in the next few days. Jennifer had grown up in the San Fernando Valley, and was now living in Torrance – I was in Redondo Beach at the time – and Mimmie was staying with her for a few days en route to Hawaii where she was going to live with Paula.

Talk about a shocker.

Patt and I wound up taking Mimmie and Jennifer to lunch at the restaurant where Jennifer was a hostess, and I think I wound up taking Mimmie to the airport a few days later. But more importantly, I realized Jennifer and I should be friends, or at least cousins who cared about each other.

And before long, that started a re-connection with her mother, Paula, who quickly returned to my life as my closest relative and remains so to this day.

A little history.

When I was nine years old, I attended Paula's wedding. I was heart-broken. I thought my 16-year-old cousin, youngest in her family, was going to wait for me to grow up so we could date. Many years later, I learned that Paula wasn't waiting for anything, and was hurrying to get married, because she was pregnant – with Jennifer.

Flash ahead a decade or so, and Paula and then husband Leon were living in the Valley, with their four kids (two other girls and a young boy), while I was growing up and getting ready for college, the newspaper world, or the Navy. It must have been about 1966.

Paula had called me and wanted me to meet a young friend of hers, Gloria Rockefeller – amazing how I can remember names and situations a half-century later. I was probably 17 years old and was driving, and the L.A. freeways were free, and free-flowing. It was nothing to drive from Santa Monica to the Valley. Gloria was living with Paula at the time, and we dated for a stretch.

One night, Gloria and I were necking on the couch when Paula's husband, Leon, came out to send me home and play responsible adult. Ah, the irony. Gloria was older than Paula had been when she got pregnant with their first daughter.

But returning to the point: I only knew Jennifer, my second cousin, as the oldest of a batch of kids. She might have been 10 or 11 when I was dating Gloria.

Now we flash ahead another 10 or 12 years and she's calling to rip into me for not coming to see Mimmie. Maybe because she was right. Or because she was Paula's daughter. Who knows? I took the tongue-lashing and jumped to attention.

Soon after, Jennifer and I were spending time together. I wound up taking my daughter Lisa to Hawaii for a visit about the time Jennifer was moving there, and the three of us spent a week sightseeing and hanging out together.

My relationships with both Paula and Jennifer blossomed in the 1980s, to where I made several trips to Hawaii. A few years later, when Jennifer was living in Sweetwater, Texas, I arranged a business trip to visit in the days before her wedding.

I did not actually attend the wedding, which was on a Sunday, because I had other items on my agenda. I was covering the Rams in those days, and they were scheduled to play the Houston Oilers (Coach Bum Phillips, star running back Earl Campbell) in the Astrodome that day. Before the wedding and football game, I routed myself to Amarillo, Texas, via Dallas. Then drove to Sweetwater. On Saturday, I flew from Amarillo to Dallas, to Houston, in time for the game.

I missed the wedding, but enjoyed time with Paula and Jennifer and the rest of their family in the days before the event.

Now I was reconnected with the one branch of my family that I felt pretty good about. I later connected briefly with Paula's older sisters, Violet and Ruby. The latter remains an email friend although we have not actually seen each other in decades.

When Mimmie passed away in Kailua, Hawaii, in her early 90s, Paula arranged a wonderful ceremony that I was able to attend. Her ashes were carried to sea on an outrigger canoe rowed by members of a local canoe club, with Paula, Jennifer and me on board. We then cast her adrift, along with appropriate flowers and all said a few words.

It was the kind of memorial ceremony I could appreciate, especially at a time when I was pretty much anti-funeral.

Paula also put together a family reunion in 1996 when she was living in New Mexico. That's an easy date to remember, since daughter Allie was a three-month-old hamster for that trip. At that event, I got to meet another long-lost cousin, Carol Walker (now Hampton).

Grandmother Mimmie had three children, hence three branches of the family. Her oldest daughter, Ruby, was parent to Violet, Little Ruby and Paula. I have very minimal memories of the older two.

In addition to my mother, Lorena (Rena), there was uncle Clyde. He was the church deacon and insurance salesman who seemed to represent the religious branch of the family. Cousins Carol and Joani were always thrown together with Ronnie and me for birthdays in the 1950s and into the 60s, since they all had January birthdays. We never did celebrate on my birthday, Dec. 30. Another lifelong hang-up. Later on, the Walkers had a third child — perhaps a major "whoops" since he was at least 10 years after the fact.

I saw Carol and her new husband at that reunion in 1996, and we exchange Christmas cards.

Joani remained a distant memory — someone I probably last saw in the early 1960s, until my son, Randy, moved to McCall, Idaho, to work at Brundage Ski Area. While on a ski visit there, he introduced me to Joani Labrousse, who was a ski area volunteer host along with her husband. Joani had left her family for Idaho at an early age and led a very interesting life, before winding up in McCall.

I got to know her briefly then, spending a couple of hours reminiscing, and realized she was the smart one — she got out of California as soon as she could and moved to Idaho. She had several careers, and raised a family. She and her husband seem to be living a rich outdoor life in Idaho.

Of all the cousins, it seems that Joani (now in Idaho), and Paula (now in New Mexico) and I might have the most in common.

Tracing a little bit of the family lineage, Mildred Krause (Mimmie) and her three children, Ruby, Rena and Clyde, are all deceased, as are all of their spouses. Of Ruby's children, Little Ruby is alive in the Silicon Valley of California and Paula is in New Mexico. I am Rena's lone surviving child. All three of Clyde's children are alive: Carol in Oregon, Joani in Idaho, and James in Southern California.

I can do little to trace the heritage on my father's side. I know that his parents, Fred and Mattie Cox, raised three daughters and two sons in rural Aurora, Nebraska, in the early 1900s. My father, Kenny, was born in 1906, "too young to serve in the first war and too old for the second," I remember him saying.

133

His sisters were Hazel, Hattie and Beulah. We were around each of their families briefly during our years in Idaho (1959-62), but there were no close connections. My dad was the youngest sibling, and I was part of his second family, so all of my cousins were 20 or more years older than me.

As close as I became to Jennifer – and as thankful as I was for that chastising phone call – we drifted apart. She went through several husbands, in Texas, then wound up moving to New Mexico, and dropping from sight. Paula shared the news that she had become a bit of a hermit, and passed away from a combination of bad life choices.

She was very important for bringing me back into the family fold, and I will always appreciate her for that.

GAMBLING (CIRCA 1975-82)

The date of Oct. 18, 1975 should be etched in my memory as one of the most important in my life. It isn't.

I had to look it up, although that wasn't hard, because I knew where to look. I knew it was a fall Monday night in about 1975, and I knew the Patriots were thrashing the Jets on Monday Night Football.

It was the day when my career as a compulsive gambler should have ended, but didn't. I had become an obsessive football gambler in barely a year. It was the classic path, from the parlay cards (pick three, four or more winners against the spread) to straight game betting. I had followed the path, from $5 or $10 on the weekly parlay cards, which promised payoffs of 10 or 15 to 1, to trying to pick one winner.

It's easy to debunk the Reefer Madness theory of that era, which preached there was an express lane from smoking marijuana to mainlining heroin. But for those prone to compulsive and addictive behavior, football betting offered a clear path from parlay cards to serious gambling, and many football fans followed it.

My expertise on college and pro football was going to reward me on a regular basis. Somebody in Las Vegas said the Rams should beat the Seahawks by 7½ points. All you had to do was pick Rams minus 7½ points or Seahawks plus 7½ points. You wagered 11 dollars to win 10. Easy money.

Minimum bet with most bookies in those days was $50 a game. But it was easy to blow past that to $100 a game, since you did not have to actually hand over the money before the game. Bookies took bets on credit.

It's a lot easier to call in a handful of bets ranging in size from a half dollar ($50), to a dollar ($100), to a dime ($1,000). You could also bet on two games at once and if you connected, the payoff was 13 to 5. There were many other exotic combinations, including the aptly named "teasers," which allowed you to move the pointspread.

This supermarket of sports excitement was available on your telephone every week, from Thursday night through Monday night. Tuesday was settle-up day.

Tuesday, Oct. 19, 1975 would have been the settle-up day of all time, had not the Patriots pounded the Jets mercilessly. I had thrown good money after bad, with good judgment quickly taking a hike as well, over that previous weekend. My losses were about $880 at the end of the Sunday afternoon games (no Sunday night games in 1975).

I had all day Monday to study the game between the Pats and the Jets and make the bet of my young lifetime. I was going to plunge eight dollars ($800) on one team and I had to be right. I had no idea where I was going to come up with more than $1,700 on Tuesday if I was wrong.

I thought I might be able to go to the credit union, or Beneficial Finance or …. I don't know what I thought. I guess I believed I was going to get it right.

The bookie I used in those early days of my gambling, Sam (no last names) established a routine with me when I first started gambling with him. His collection guy, whose name I can't remember, would show up at the *Daily Breeze* newsroom on Tuesday afternoon. He was young and looked like he could have been a football player had he used his calories better. But he also had a rough edge to him. You knew he represented danger.

On many of those early Tuesdays, he was bringing me my winnings (perhaps $150 or 200), or collecting a sum that never reached that amount. I was drifting outside my economic zip code. In 1975, I might have been earning $300 a week, before taxes.

It was so easy to speak into the phone, and say, "I'll take a dollar on the Rams minus 7½," and list several other games without registering that was more than a week's pay. And that was just the morning games. If you were losing your morning bets, you started working on the afternoon games, and often that meant increasing your bets.

The picture should be easy to clarify: The opportunities for self-destruction built through the weekend. College games Saturday morning, afternoon and evening; NFL games Sunday morning and afternoon, and the big Monday night game as everybody tried to get even.

Little wonder why the NFL has expanded to Thursday and Sunday nights, knowing the legalized gambling is now available in more states than not. One big positive for legalized sports gambling over working with a bookie like Sam: You have to pay your money out front.

Normally, a Patriots-Jets game in October would be of little interest to fans in Suburban Los Angeles. But Monday Night Football was still a cultural event in the 1970s. The group I hung around with, mostly single teachers but a few others, rotated the Monday Night game around and it was a party as well as a sports event.

Many in the crowd were casually invested in the game, maybe a $10 parlay card, or a $5 friendly wager based on somebody's region of origin. I know for certain that nobody was an invested as I was that night. The Patriots were favored by 13½ points, a large spread. That meant the game started with the Jets ahead 13½ to 0 in the computers of all gamblers. Fortunately, the Pats started scoring early, and often on the inept team in green.

Most in the viewing audience stopped caring when it was 20 or 27 to nothing. But I was locked in. I had seen games where one coach had an insurmountable lead and allowed a couple of seemingly meaningless late scores, or "technical touchdowns," which altered the betting outcome.

I was cheering like a madman until the final gun, surely the only one at the party who cared about the final score.

It meant the difference between staving off disaster – financial ruin – and living the play another day. As it was, because of the mechanics of the wager, I wound up owing Sam a few bucks when it was done, perhaps $50 or $60. But I was thrilled to be paying that, instead of the $1,700 that I did not have.

That was the game that should have cured me of betting on football.

Fat chance. With my addictive personality, that trip to the edge of the cliff, and the peek over the edge, just fanned the flames. I was so hooked.

Granted, I had some expertise in pro football from the mid-1970s through the 1980s and into the '90s. I covered the Rams from 1975 to 1981, and the Raiders from 1982 through 1994. I was around the players, coaches and administrative staff of these teams. I had an insider's knowledge about who was hot and who was not, about who might be nursing a sore ankle, or a more serious injury.

I should also have known which coaches were likely to run up the score on a divisional opponent, and who might not care about covering the spread. And I was picking NFL games against the spread in a weekly column in *The Daily Breeze* that ran every Sunday for 20 years.

For many of those years, I had a mystery picker who I competed against, called Coach X. Since the NFL had a clear policy against anything gambling – although the league knew its success was tied to the gambling – Coach X had to remain anonymous. He was usually an assistant coach, often on the team I covered, although one year Coach X was a head coach, and another year he was an assistant general manager. Coaches and players were supposed to be oblivious to the pointspread, but I can assure you they weren't.

When the Rams went to their first Super Bowl after the 1979 season, it was after a 9-0 victory over the Bucs in Tampa, and many were aware that one writer cashed his biggest ever bet on that game because Coach X had told him, "There is no flippin' way they can score on our defense. All we've got to do is kick a couple field goals and not throw any interceptions."

Coach X called a masterful game and made sure his quarterback wasn't in a position to throw interceptions. That game was worth two dimes to me ($2,000), and I was on top of my betting game that night. Coach X that year was the head coach of the winning team, which was favored by three points, as I recall.

But inside knowledge only works once in a while. Over the years, neither Coach X nor I was spectacularly successful against the pointspread, the great leveler of all sports betting. Most years, we were both around 54 to 55 percent winners. Often it was closer to 50 percent. And math majors will tell you that betting 11 to win 10, you need to win 55 percent of the time to break even.

The more games you bet, the more that 10 percent edge (or juice) adds up against you. And if you become hooked, you start thinking you can have insights into games that others don't. Yeah, right.

Ultimately, you spend most weeks trying to get back to even, as I did on that night in 1975. I had winning weeks and winning seasons, for the most part. But I also had drama, and I also had some down moments.

I never had to take out a second mortgage on the house, or borrow money, but the series of highs and lows that is sports gambling began to wear on me. By the 1980s, I was starting to realize I was working way too hard to break even.

There was no moment, or no day, when I just woke up and decided to quit cold turkey. Like so many gamblers, I believed I had an edge, and a chance to win. I just wasn't enjoying the winning as much as I was dreading the losing.

And there was one other aspect that started in the 1970s and was a potential career disaster as well. I was covering the Rams, who were coached by Chuck Knox, and were a very good team in those days. They were good enough to be favored in most games, but not always good enough to cover the spread.

As a sports writer covering the team, your calling card is your objectivity. Yet it's hard to get on the team plane after a 14-10 comeback win when you were betting the Rams to win minus 5 points. You lose the bet, and probably more than a day's salary, yet you needed to write about the positive aspects of the win.

That was probably one of a dozen reasons I continued to work on my addiction to Scotch whisky at the same time.

When I quit betting football, it wasn't something I announced, or wrote about in a column. I just decided to limit myself to picking games in the paper. The highs weren't as high but the lows weren't as low.

I did not vow to give up gambling entirely. I still enjoy playing Blackjack when I'm in a casino, and buy a few squares on a Super Bowl numbers board. But those are things I can control better than a running back fumbling the ball to set up a technical touchdown and snatch pointspread defeat from the jaws of victory.

COVERING THE SUPER
BOWL RAMS (1979)

In the spring of 1979, news of the death of Carroll Rosenbloom was a national story. The 72-year-old owner of the Rams died while swimming in the ocean off Golden Beach in Florida.

Widespread rumors surfaced about a mysterious Canadian swimmer in the ocean with Rosenbloom. And stories abounded that his heart attack was caused by an electronic prod under the water. But nothing was ever proved.

South Bay attorney Tony Capozzola showed me a picture of the pre-cremation body of C.R. that he said showed something in the eyes to indicate the shock. But C.R. was cremated within 24 hours of his death, at the wishes of wife Georgia Rosenbloom.

Then came the rest of the story.

First, from the perspective of a sports writer covering the Rams, was how it would affect the management of the team. C.R., as Rosenbloom was widely known, was a bon vivant and man who enjoyed life in Southern California. He had traded ownership of the legendary Baltimore Colts for the Rams years earlier to a buffoon named Robert Irsay. He then brought in Chuck Knox as coach, and the Rams became one of the best teams in the NFL.

C.R. was the owner and his two primary executives were Don Klosterman and Steve Rosenbloom, C.R.'s son. Klosterman was another man about town but highly regarded in NFL circles. Steve Rosenbloom had been apprenticing to run the Rams since he was a ball boy and worked as an assistant to the equipment manager as a child. He was also the kind of "get it done" guy that everyone loves. When the team bus driver put his vehicle in a situation he could not handle, down a dead-end street on a dark night in Philadelphia, it was Steve who took over the wheel and got the vehicle turned around and drove it to the hotel.

Steve was also the maestro, along with defensive coordinator Ray Malavasi, of the hero sandwiches that the two created on the team charter plane for flights to the east.

Steve was also my best friend among the Rams' hierarchy. He was the kind of guy who would be out drinking beers in Hermosa Beach, with wife Renee, during the week. And it was widely expected that he would be running the team after his father's passing.

Nothing appeared to change that thinking when the will was read after the death.

Nobody ever equated wealth with wisdom. Or common sense.

C.R. left 70 percent of the team to wife Georgia, and six percent each to Steve and his two siblings from the first marriage, as well as two half-siblings born out of wedlock to C.R. and Georgia.

The model for leaving the majority of the team to the wife was the San Francisco 49ers, where the same happened and the widow sat in the owner's box and let the professionals run the team.

That lasted less than four months. Georgia fired Steve as executive vice president and left the running of the team to Klosterman. This was the year of turmoil on other fronts.

Before his death, C.R. had allowed Knox – the most successful coach in Rams history and winner of five straight NFC West Division titles – to leave for the Buffalo Bills. Knox was known as Ground Chuck for his run-oriented offense. And he had one of the most smothering defenses in the NFL. But they did not win with flair – often not covering the pointspread which was important to C.R.'s friends in the entertainment industry – and they did not win the NFC title game to advance to the Super Bowl.

So, another legendary coach, George Allen, was brought out of retirement to supply the magic touch. Except that on a team where eccentricity was the norm, he was truly eccentric. His multiple rules for training camp, including a rigid order about what foods were where in the buffet line at the Cal State Fullerton cafeteria – ran afoul of senior players, who complained to management.

This was also the end of the era where coaches withheld water, and water breaks, from players during the heat of summer training camp. They also believed in excessive training to the detriment of players' health. But Allen's worst sin, in all likelihood, was his belief that as coach, he was the master of the domain. He wasn't interested in input from management. And he lost a couple of exhibition games in boring fashion.

While her late husband had the patience and the experience to realize that two weeks in August were not pivotal in the overall scheme of things, Georgia was impatient and wanted action.

Allen was fired after two preseason games, and the team's veteran defensive coordinator, Malavasi, was named head coach. Except Malavasi had staved off his own departure earlier by accepting an unheard of transfer to offensive coordinator, so that Bud Carson could become defensive coordinator. Carson came from the Steelers and was widely credited with crafting the famed Steel Curtain Defense.

Malavasi was a great coach – defensive ends Fred Dryer and Jack Youngblood would swear to this day he was the reason for the successes of 1979. But he was not great on public relations and usually said what he was thinking, even when it included four-letter words and threatening behavior.

But the Rams won in 1979 – using three quarterbacks who are not in the Hall of Fame – and were on the verge of their first-ever Super Bowl. They went to Tampa for the NFC title game, and beat the Bucs (coached by John McKay), 9-0, in a defensive battle.

A Rams vs. Steelers Super Bowl was on the nation's mind that Sunday night in January of 1980 after the game.

The Rams flew United Airlines charters to away games, and because C.R. like to travel in comfort on his own dime, he paid a little extra to guarantee they were on the stretch version of the venerable DC-8, which had been in service for years.

In this model, there were four seats in front of the galley and immediately behind the cockpit, two facing backward and two facing forward. And a table dropped down between them. This was where the four senior sports writers sat on the flight home, because we could work on our portable typewriters on this table, and not disturb those in first class, or the players back in the elongated economy class. Players often had a row of three seats to themselves, but were guaranteed at least three seats for every two players.

Remember this was year's before TSA, strict airline and airport security, screening of luggage and so many other things we take for granted. Also, back when the overhead storage was a rack, not a bin.

When the Rams and other sports teams would land at an airport, they would park on the tarmac, and the 3 or 4 charter buses would drive out to the planes. Players and staff would go down the stairway and right onto the bus. And when departing, the reverse was true. So, when there was a delay that kept us on the ground in Tampa for 90 minutes or so, we sat on the tarmac with the door open. And the four writers in the front of the plane – I was in the back-facing aisle seat – could look out the open doorway.

The delay had nothing to do with the plane, or air travel, or even the loading of team luggage, which was substantial for a football team. We were waiting The Tickets.

Again, time frame. There were no computer-generated tickets in those days. Tickets were printed by the NFL and the distribution of Super Bowl tickets was one of the most important aspects of the two weeks before the game. Each of the participating teams received about one-fourth of the tickets for the game to be held at the Rose Bowl. That meant the Rams were to get about 26,000 tickets for the then 104,000-seat Rose Bowl.

These were to be used to satisfy season-ticket holders, sponsors, advertisers, friends in the know, etc. And most NFL owners probably moved a few tickets into the resale market (scalping) since these were hard to track. The NFL kept a lid on prices, selling all tickets to every Super Bowl for the same price. For the game to be played after the 1979 season (in January 1980), that price was $100. Which meant they could instantly be scalped for two- or three-times face value.

How many season ticket holders got seats? How many re-sold them? This was a story the NFL never commented on. Then or now.

I was involved twice, with the Rams in '79 and the Raiders in '83, and know that sports writers often got a chance to purchase tickets, too. These often were re-sold at market value, which was considerably more than face value.

So, the movement of 26,000 tickets was an important issue. And Georgia Rosenbloom's companion, her accompanist as he was introduced to us, was award-winning composer Dominic Frontiere. When NFL officials handed the Rams this package of gold, 26,000 tickets – worth easily triple their face value of $100 each – they were given to Frontiere.

Later, he would marry Georgia, giving her the seventh married name of her life. He would also be indicted for and convicted of tax evasion and fraud and served a number of months in federal prison for his role in the ticket scalping. The government charged him with making $500,000 profit on the 16,000 tickets he sold. Frontiere took the fall for Georgia, who divorced him while he was incarcerated.

But the major moment of that delay on the tarmac in Tampa was between Georgia Rosenbloom and me, although it was never reported in any publication.

When she fired Steve in the summer before that magical season, *The Daily Breeze* was privy to a lot of inside information because of my relationship with Steve Rosenbloom. Were the stories negative to Georgia? No more than any story with one golden inside source. Except there were two sources, Steve's then wife Renee was also known to make late-night calls to her favorite sports writer to share information.

So, when the Rams went on the road, Georgia made it a conscious effort never to speak to me during that entire season. We might pass in the aisle on the plane, or in the lobby of the hotel, or in the press box at a game, but she would always avert her eyes. Never so much as nodding or acknowledging. Which was perfectly appropriate and certainly did not bother me.

But on that Sunday night after the biggest win in team history, she was working her way around the airplane in Tampa while sipping victory champagne. And after an hour or so of hugging players, coaches, and executives, she started to share her happiness with the writers.

When she had worked her to way to that card-table seating arrangement at the front, we were pounding away on stories on our portable typewriters.

Then she sat on the lap of Joe Hendrickson, the jolly senior columnist from the *Pasadena Star News,* who was known as The Senator. Joe loved the attention and the affection. Georgia was a woman in her mid-50s who took very good care of herself. She wore her expensive sweaters very well, showcasing her widely believed-to-be-equally expensive breasts.

I had a few moments to think about how I might handle an unfortunate moment. When she got off The Senator's lap and tried to sit on mine in the same affectionate moment, I tried to keep typing, but when she was clearly going to interrupt, I used my right forearm on her back and gently pushed her away, saying, "Georgia, I'm busy writing my story."

Wearing high heels, no doubt expensive ones, and showing the effects of quite a bit of champagne, she stumbled as she tried to correct the aborted landing on my lap. One of her aides caught her and steered her back to her first-class seat, where she finished the champagne while waiting for Dominic and The Tickets.

The Senator chastised me for not letting her sit on my lap, but I explained that she had not spoken to me since firing Steve. And I didn't feel very affectionate at the time. Besides, I was trying to make a 9-0 game sound exciting.

When the 1980 season arrived, the Rams quietly let it be known to the newspaper sports world that they would no longer be flying the DC-8 charters – cost was hinted as the reason – and would be flying on smaller planes. And sports writers would not be accommodated as guests on the team flights. Was I to blame? I'd like to think so.

At a time when Watergate reporting was bringing down a president, and when newspapers were climbing out of the pockets of politicians and others, they were being forced to pay the way for their writers. Like so many things in my life, it turned out great. United and American Airlines started their frequent flyer programs in 1982, and before long, every sports writer in America was talking about mileage point accruals.

Did you know that during the height of the competition, you could get 500 miles for the shortest of flights – say LAX to San Diego – and the airlines were tripling miles to 1,500 miles one way? I flew to San Diego games several years in a row and reaped the benefit of 3,000 miles for a 250-mile round trip.

SPORTS WRITING SCOOPS
(1981 & LATER)

Once you get past reporting the news, and covering sports is mostly just that, you realize it's a very competitive job. You and a dozen other reporters (in the 1970s and '80s and into the '90s) were attending a game, and each of you was putting your own perspective on the same set of basic facts. No getting around who won, how they won, who were the star players, what did the players and coaches say about the game? Basic stuff. But each of us had a different viewpoint, and that's why I loved picking up five or six papers the day after a game to see not how the Rams did, but how the other writers did. And how I fared in the daily competition.

I was always judging myself, sometimes quite harshly, and wondering if anybody else was noticing the differences.

But there was a higher level of reporting, and that was truly the joy I started embracing as I matured into my work. That would be breaking the news or being the first to report something significant. Old-school journalists would call it a scoop. Later the phrase was refined to "The Guy Who Broke That Story." When we were mostly a news world based on print journalism, it was a great competition judged on what you published in your newspaper.

And if you broke the news, the others had to credit you as they played "catch-up" the next day. There was no greater joy in the 1970s and early

'80s than seeing a story in the *L.A. Times,* that included the line, "as first reported in the Torrance *Daily Breeze."* Nine times out of ten, that meant either me (Rams and later Raiders) or Chris Mortensen (Dodgers) had gotten the scoop. It was an informal but ongoing competition.

Then we evolved into around-the-clock electronic journalism – spell that ESPN if you've forgotten – and news could be broken at any time of day or night. In addition to the electronic media jumping into the competition, newspapers were posting stories on web sites, playing to the 24-hour clock.

My first major scoop, and perhaps my biggest, came in 1981 and surprisingly, it didn't even come on my beat. I'd always believed – and still do – that breaking the news requires building relationships with as many players, coaches and front office staffers as you can. Better yet, a relationship with the owner (as I had for most but not all the Raiders' years in L.A.) trumps almost everything else. Earlier, I had a great relationship with Coach Ray Malavasi of the Rams, as well as owners' son and General Manager Steve Rosenbloom. But those led to only minor scoops.

In June of 1981, my roommate and fellow staff writer Mortensen wanted a couple of weeks at home about the time his beat, the Dodgers, required him to head to the road for a trip that was scheduled for Chicago, St. Louis and Pittsburgh. I was covering the Angels at home only, so he proposed a swap, and the higher powers agreed. I had done a few Dodger road trips in the 1970s and enjoyed the baseball lifestyle.

We headed east, knowing that this trip might get cut short because the baseball players – then growing into strength as a union – were threatening a strike. And the owners were doing little to prevent it. There was little major reporting being done about the rattling of swords from both sides regarding the strike. Truth is, nobody in sports journalism was very skilled in labor reporting in those days.

Anyway, I headed to Chicago knowing only that I would be on the Dodgers' charter plane for as long as the season continued before the strike. And would likely get a ride home if and when the players did go on strike. Sports labor wars were in their infancy in those days, and we were learning as we went along.

The joy – and the headache – of any trip to Chicago for the Dodger writers was that Wrigley Field did not have lights in those days. All day games. Chicago had some of the greatest nightlife in North America and the bars stayed open until 4 a.m. No wonder veteran baseball writer Gordy Verrell said of a trip to the Windy City: "Chicago took me two falls out of three. But it was a great loss."

A half dozen writers were in a thriving bar after the second game of the trip on a Saturday. This was the height of the sexual revolution, of a freestyle approach to meeting members of the opposite sex that was a nightly challenge. One of the younger writers wanted to approach one of the best-looking women at the bar, and the table immediately discussed two categories of women in that bar: Writers Types and Players Types. My friend had aspirations to get to know a Players Type. Great chance to waste time and money and nearly a guaranteed loss. She was looking to meet Steve Garvey or Reggie Smith or one of the other Dodgers. Not Chris Who of the Daily What?

So, the writer asked for clarification: What was a Writers Type? Rather than tell him about a Writers Type, I would show him. There is a fairly basic description: A Writers Type is a Players Type with eight- or 10-years' experience. Perhaps a little short of homecoming queen, and no longer 22 or 23 years old.

Anyway, I got up to go chat with the best visual description I could find. I did not return to the writers table for the rest of the night. My guess was correct, and I quickly hit it off with my new friend. After a few drinks, we left the loud bar for a quiet spot, and continued to grow the relationship. Next morning, I scampered back to the team hotel, and after packing for the bus to the Sunday game, I called the Dodgers' traveling secretary.

All teams had an administrator who traveled with the team and made sure everything worked as it was supposed to. Among his duties was managing the stash of tickets the home team gives to the visiting team. Happens in all sports. Players grew up in an area, have family or friends who want to attend the game. Or writers meet new friends the night before in a Rush Street bar in Chicago.

Lee Scott was the traveling secretary and he was happy to leave two tickets for my friend, Lynn, at the Press Will Call window. After setting up in the press box and doing pre-game interview work, I came out to sit in the stands with Lynn. One key aspect of Writers Types is that they can carry on a conversation and might even have a brain in their head.

Since the Dodgers were leaving after the game on chartered busses to the airport, followed by a short flight to St. Louis, I figured the five or six innings I spent sitting with Lynn would be the last time I saw her until my next trip to Chicago, whenever that might be.

But since Lynn was a baseball fan, our conversation circled around the impending strike. And then she mentioned she worked for a re-insurance company. In truth, I had never heard of re-insurance and was barely able to make my auto premium payments to Farmers Insurance. When I asked what re-insurance companies did, Lynn explained that they worked with companies who were insuring a risk, and bought some of the action, for a price.

"Like baseball's strike insurance," she said. Now I may have been sort of listening and sort of paying attention to the game, but now she had my attention. Turns out Lynn's company had looked at baseball's strike insurance policy and chosen not to buy any of the risk. Lynn's boss made the decision.

Since the existence of a strike insurance policy was rumored but not-yet confirmed, this was news.

Lynn had seen the policy that would pay baseball owners handsomely if the players went on strike, and she was conversant in it. I was hooked.

"Can you get a copy of the policy?" I asked. "Sure, there's one in my desk," she said.

When the Dodgers-Cubs game ended – the world will little know or care who won – we had agreed that she would go into the office, copy the strike insurance policy, and fly to St. Louis to bring it to me. Those were the days when you could walk up to an airline counter, buy a ticket, and be on a flight minutes later.

So, I filed my game story, and packed up for the trip to St. Louis. But I also called my boss and said I might have a major story later that night and to plan for space on the front page of sports. After thinking about it, he said it was bigger than that and talked to the editor about a spot on the front page of the newspaper.

If the robber barons who owned baseball teams had taken out a policy to reward them in the event of a strike, there was no reason to settle with the players, and there would be no more baseball after the strike deadline, which was looming on Wednesday.

I got to my room in St. Louis, set up my portable typewriter, and the device we used to send pages electronically back to the office (called a Xerox telecopier) and waited for my new best friend. A few hours later, Lynn arrived – having gone to the office, copied a 30-page document, and bought a plane ticket to St. Louis on her own dime with no promise of reimbursement. While I read the policy, I happily rewarded her with the best steak room service had to offer.

I was able to make sense of the policy, with Lynn's help, and wrote a story that shocked the nation's sports fans. While most of us thought the owners would do what it took to prevent a strike, they had done what rich people usually do – they insured themselves against a negative outcome. In fact, owners of many teams would do better during a strike than while games were being played. No salaries to pay to players but income would continue from the insurance and re-insurance policies.

I wrote a story that was picked up by the wire services and every major paper in the country, and each of them attributed it to *The Daily Breeze*, in Torrance, California.

Lynn decided to stay in St. Louis for a day, and we enjoyed our growing relationship.

A day later, baseball's union made it official. The Players were on strike. As per management's plan, players who were on the road with their teams were on their own.

This made for an interesting situation, since many players had never traveled on their own. Teams and traveling secretaries took care of all arrangements. Many of the players were young and didn't even have credit cards or enough money to buy a plane ticket home. Veterans like Rick Monday and Steve Yeager were at St. Louis airport, helping young players get tickets home and, in some cases, putting them on their personal Master Card or Visa.

The Dodgers flew their team plane home with only the manager, his coaches, trainers and a few other staffers, and the traveling writers. It was a very empty plane.

Back in Torrance, my new beat was the baseball strike, and I called Lynn and she continued to assist me in finding insights worthy of national stories.

Months later, when she was in Los Angeles on re-insurance business and staying at the Bonaventure, I took her out to dinner at the hotel's fanciest restaurant. When I submitted the $100-plus tab (remember, this was 1981), Sports Editor Mike Waldner balked at paying the expense. I explained that a series of national scoops was well worth the price. He seemed to think I also gained something personal out of the event – "you got laid" was the blunt version – and declined to submit the tab. Being a resourceful fellow, however, I was able to find a way for the Breeze to pay the tab. And, yes, he was right. But I didn't think that was the point.

Over the years, there were other scoops of varying degrees of national or regional import. Things like the Raiders drafting a running back from the Naval Academy in the fourth round – but paying him first round money because they knew he would be able to play for them after a deal Al Davis had made with the Secretary of the Navy to station the player in Long Beach on a ship in drydock.

The hiring and firing of coaches were usually a great chance for a news break, if you worked your contacts right. And after all, that's what the news business was about. That and knowing the difference between a Players Type and a Writers Type.

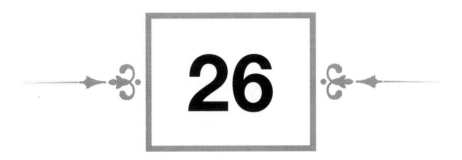

CONDO ON PROSPECT, ROOMMATES (1981-1985)

My relationship with Patt Robinson (1978-81) involved buying a condo together in North Redondo, so when it came time to dissolve things, I was looking for a place to live.

Sharon Blanks was a real estate salesperson who was briefly a friend, and at that time, she was connected with a lot of developers who had projects coming on the market in the recession.

Her plan: If I could find another buyer, she would partner with me in a new unit on Prospect in South Redondo. When Melinda Anderson, a friend of Patt's, saw what a good deal it was, she jumped in.

I had first choice of the 14 units, and picked the one in the back that overlooked the jacuzzi, was closest to the barbecue, and looked out on the old Torrance Drive-in from the master bedroom. When Melinda looked at the project, that was her choice, too, but it was taken. She took the one on the opposite end of that building.

For the next two years, she and I were the only occupants of the 14-unit complex.

Four years later, I met Nancy and when she moved in, my life changed for the better in every way possible. But for four years, the Prospect condo was the greatest party place I could imagine.

There were a couple of female roommates in the early years.

One of them took the best approach I'd ever heard to roommates of the opposite sex getting along. Over dinner while getting to know one another, she offered this proposition: Let's go to bed together tonight and deal with the curiosity. That way we can live in separate bedrooms and never wonder about the other person.

I liked that thinking. And she stuck to her plan, by the way.

The best-ever roommate was Chris Mortensen, who covered the Dodgers for *The Daily Breeze* and was one of the most fun people I have ever known. For most of our time as roomies, he was breaking stories on the Dodger beat and I was dominating the Rams and then the Raider beats. If the *Times* had to credit *The Daily Breeze* as source of a story, it was a slam dunk that it came out of the condo on Prospect.

Mort wound up leaving for the Atlanta *Journal-Constitution* and later the short-lived *The National*, and started breaking stories on both baseball and football. He wound up with a national book about scandals in college football recruiting, and moved to ESPN where he still works.

But the best memories of Mort aren't work related.

In 1982, the NFL started its season, then went on strike. I had torn the cartilage in my right knee playing softball before going to training camp. When the strike appeared to be lasting, I had surgery.

I wound up with a full-length cast on my right leg, which was a bit of a challenge in a condo that has three levels.

When baseball ended, and the NFL strike was progressing, Mort and I started a Sunday routine that we continued throughout the strike. We'd head off to a restaurant called Pancho & Wong's for Sunday Brunch. Then we'd hang out until we had collected a party – maybe around 3 or 4 in the afternoon – then we'd bring them all back to the condo for a barbecue and jacuzzi party.

Years later, I met people who remembered those parties.

One of the things they remembered was the giant yellow rubber device I used to cover my cast so I could hang out in the jacuzzi. Since that was all I was wearing, mostly, it drew attention. The early 1980s were a continuation of the lifestyle that included very few rules.

Mort was a collector of friends in those days, so Sundays weren't our only parties. They were just our biggest and most memorable.

In 1985, Nancy moved in, and in 1987, we were married. We continued to live in the condo through the birth of both children, before moving to our house in 1996.

The details of ownership in that condo were fuzzy for a time. After Sharon's departure, I made only partial payments to the developers, then no payments for a while. Eventually, Melinda and I hired an attorney to sort out our deal with the developers that worked to both of our benefit. Then Sharon reappeared and wanted to experience her share of what could be a windfall.

For a time, she was using an attorney on the 10th floor of the giant building on Hawthorne Blvd, and I was using an attorney on the 14th. Whenever they'd exchange proposals, the attorneys would call a delivery service and bill Sharon and me $50 or $75. That and their hourly billing fees was bleeding us both.

Finally, I threw in the towel, and we paid Sharon $30k to relinquish full title. That cleared the way for the move to Onrado Street in 1996. When I left behind that condo, there were a lot of great memories.

SANTA ROSA WITH THE
RAIDERS (1982-84)

The Raiders' decision to abandon Oakland (the first time) and move to L.A. was the best thing that could have happened to me, journalistically and career wise.

After a lengthy court battle that was hard to follow, it was clear the NFL could not stop maverick owner Al Davis from moving his team if he wanted, and had a viable suitor. He had not yet sealed a stadium deal – his great hope – but the L.A. Memorial Coliseum was a step up from the Oakland-Alameda County Coliseum. Although both were aged edifices, L.A.'s stadium had 40,000 more seats, and no baseball tenant, so the first four to six games did not have to be played with dirt on much of the field.

But those were minor details. The Raiders were coming at a time when the Rams had lost their luster just three years into the Reign of Queen Georgia. They had played well but lost to Pittsburgh in the 1979 Super Bowl, but were paying the price for bad decisions on personnel and coaching. Their fan base had shifted to Orange County since the move to Anaheim Stadium, and the vast majority of L.A. that was not Orange County was thirsty for a new team.

From a personal point of view, all the pieces were falling into place for a new beat. The new team would renovate and rent a closed school site in El Segundo for their headquarters, which made them the South Bay's team. They were only a year removed from a Super Bowl win and they had a roster full of the best stories in sports.

Logistically, the daily drive would be 15 or 20 minutes each way instead of 45 to 60.

It started in Santa Rosa, in July of 1982, when I drove to the Raiders' training camp site at a hotel complex called the El Rancho Tropicana. They were the only team in the NFL to hold training camp at a hotel, rather than a university or college setting.

And that wasn't the only difference.

The Raiders proudly did things differently from other NFL teams on every level. During six years of covering the Rams, I had gotten used to having a P.R. man available to arrange interviews, research statistics, or provide whatever a beat writer could need. The fact is, I might have become a little soft. The NFL was the Cadillac of beats (there's a dated phrase) in 1982, and there was a reason guys who landed on pro football stayed for years. Good travel, professional help on all levels, and a game that everybody wanted to read about.

It was also the best lifestyle. Baseball writers covered a game every day, mostly on deadline; basketball writers did three or four games a week with horrible travel, and nobody cared about hockey stories. If you had the NFL beat for your paper, you had a comfortable lifestyle. You had the toughest game story of the major sports, but you only had to do it once a week. Other days were interviews with the head coach, players, plus the head coach and at least one player from the next opponent. And every other week you were traveling to an away game.

The worst part of the NFL beat was one of the best things about the NFL – Monday Night Football. After it became apparent the Raiders were not going to sell out the cavernous Coliseum (originally 93,000 seats, later reconfigured to 76,000), which meant potential blackouts of the second largest TV market in the country, it was determined the Raiders' Monday Night Games were always on the road. That meant at least one, and sometimes as many as three, MNF games, often in the eastern time zone.

Simple logistics: MNF games in the East started at 9 p.m. local time, and ended between 12;30 and 1 a.m. Which made for a harsh deadline write even for West Coast writers. And if you wanted to make the day-after press session with the head coach, you needed to be on the first jet smoking out of Miami, or Boston, or Newark, or Pittsburgh, or wherever.

Because the Raiders were a natural enemy for so many NFL teams, they were popular with the league schedule makers. It was not uncommon for two MNF games in the East in a given year. Or one at a division rival like Denver (Mountain Time Zone) or Kansas City (Central Time Zone).

The team usually whimpered about the unfairness of the NFL schedule every spring, but it was simply their reality.

For me, the Raiders were the change that re-charged my battery, starting with my first days at the El Rancho Tropicana in July of 1982.

Training camp was usually about six or seven weeks, which included at least two of the four exhibition games. Teams started with perhaps 90 candidates for their 45-man roster, practiced twice a day (although usually only once in pads), and spent early evenings in position meetings.

What I learned when I first arrived, was that the Raiders were not used to accommodating the press. There was no designated P.R. man, although several administrators filled the role on occasion. If you wanted something, you were often better asking the head coach (Tom Flores) or his administrative assistant.

The Raiders were required to post a depth chart by NFL rule, but they weren't required to update it regularly, or even keep it accurate. Rosters were minimally correct, but accuracy was not an addiction.

First lesson for the new guy covering a team: Make your own roster and check it every day – players were signed, or released on a regular basis, and the Raiders weren't keen on sharing that information. More than a few times in those first three years, I'd notice a player on the field – say, No. 24 – who was not on the roster. After practice, I'd ask Coach Tom Flores: "Oh, yeah, that's Joe Jones, he's a cornerback we signed yesterday after he was cut by the Chargers." And similarly, if a player was missing at practice, by asking you might learn he had been cut, traded, or injured. But you had to ask.

Same thing for depth charts. If you noticed a second-round draft choice who had been listed as a linebacker was suddenly playing defensive end in practice, it was up to you to update your depth chart.

Now there is nothing wrong with this. It is reporting on the most basic level, and that's why it I viewed it as a recharge of my battery. I have always loved the nuts and bolts of our business: observing, analyzing and reporting.

Another lesson was about sources: Covering a football team, you needed to have one coach on each side of the ball that you could go to for a straight answer. It was usually off the record, but he could steer you away from costly mistakes. You may have seen a safety working at linebacker and thought this was major news. Turns out it was only one minor deviation from the team's basic pass defense scheme for a certain team.

The head coach was the team spokesman, on the record, and could occasionally be your off-the-record source. But it was better to have a backup. I always started with defense, and found "my guy" there, because that was the most complex of the aspects of football to understand.

Every reporter of a certain skill set had "a guy" on both sides of the ball, and maybe somebody on the medical or training staff, or in the equipment room. And it helped if either the general manager or the personnel chief was able to answer questions for you.

With a team like the Raiders, most employees feared the wrath of owner Al Davis, so never wanted to be seen talking to a reporter.

Many reporters feared Davis as well.

But from my first days at training camp, nobody told me I couldn't walk down to the defensive side of the scrimmage – where Davis always stood – and initiate a conversation. Now Davis was not long on social amenities, so he could ignore you if he so chose. But more often than not, I was able to chat with the maverick owner. He became a major source for years, and we chatted at night – his favorite time – when he had something he wanted to leak.

Davis had always hated the dominant paper in the marketplace, wherever he was, and was not shy about leaking through an aggressive underdog paper, like *The Daily Breeze*. When he decided to take a break in his nightly weight-lifting routine, I might expect a call to talk about some "fucking this," or some "fucking that." Davis could be counted on to use that bleeping adjective at least once in every sentence most nights.

Training camp in Santa Rosa was also a great exercise in lifestyle for me. Sonoma County was not as famous as the neighboring Napa Valley for wines, but it had 40 or 50 small vineyards that produced excellent white wines. Once I found out how easy it was to visit the tasting rooms – free in those days – I was out in the community whenever the schedule allowed.

Wine tasting became my major diversion, with a specialty in Sonoma County white wines. By my second year of training camp at Santa Rosa, I became a buyer. I had about a dozen cases of wine in my hotel room by the end of camp. That pretty much filled up my Subaru, and I had to ask another writer to pack my luggage in his car for the drive home.

Women I was dating often flew up from L.A. for a weekend in Santa Rosa, which meant a chance to show off the wine tasting options, as well as some of the great dining options. Because I was on expenses, and knew how to work the system, many of them became Raider administrators or assistant coaches on the form that covered expenses.

That was before the world went to electronic submission of everything, so expenses meant filling out an extensive form each week, with a form for each day's expenses, and attaching receipts. I would then mail it to the accounting office for reimbursement.

And for the first four or five weeks of the first camp, they would mail it back to me. It wasn't the $90 dinner with Coach X, that they objected to, it was the amount of the tip. Turns out that my over-tipping triggered red lights and buzzers because Copley Newspapers had gotten into a battle with the U.S. Government several years earlier over expense account violations. We were under orders to adhere to a 15% tipping maximum in 1983. And I was a 20% guy.

They would mail the entire packet back, at a cost of maybe $8 or $9 in postage, so I could correct a $5 over-tip. Or rather, I could adjust the form so the tip conformed to the maximum and I would eat the difference. And I would pay the return postage. Eventually I got the message and conceded defeat. I would tip only the 15% maximum on the credit card, then add a little cash if the service warranted. I was a slow learner on this, but when you realize the accountants rule the world, it's a lot easier to march to their orders.

The Raiders trained in Santa Rosa for three summers, 1982, 1983 and 1984, after moving to L.A. In 1985, they relocated to Oxnard, which was about an hour to 90 minutes from home.

My last year at Santa Rosa was memorable, if only because everything was tailored around the Los Angeles Olympics. I went up to Santa Rosa for two weeks, filing daily stories, but also putting about a half-dozen features on major players in the bank, for use during the Olympics.

I was assigned to the boxing venue at the Olympics for the entire two weeks. But the newspaper was putting out a regular sports section, plus a daily 8-page Olympics Section, which included the work of top sports writers from all of the Copley papers. I was assigned boxing because that was a big year for U.S. boxing with the Soviet Bloc staying home.

A day after the Olympics ended, I was back in the Subaru for the drive north to my home away from home in Santa Rosa. I loved training camp at Santa Rosa, and while Oxnard was more convenient, I have a lot of great memories from those three years in Sonoma County.

L.A. AND THE OLYMPIC GAMES (1984)

Certainly, one of the major events in my sports writing career was the 1984 Olympic Games, in Los Angeles.

While I generally was not fond of covering big events, the Olympics was a once-in-a-lifetime opportunity.

The *Breeze* was part of the Copley Newspaper chain, which was thriving in those days. The San Diego papers (*Union in* the morning, *Tribune* in the afternoon) were the showcase, but the *Breeze* was often thought of as the next ranking paper.

While major decisions were being made all over Southern California to allow the Olympics to thrive without traffic, the Copley papers were deciding to put out a daily 8-page Olympics section that would run in all papers.

And the efforts of writers from each of the papers would be in this section.

I was designated to cover the boxing, which the editors rightly decided would be a major daily event, and often the lead story in this section.

Because the U.S. and its allies had boycotted the 1980 Games in Moscow, Russia returned the favor in 1984.

That meant boxing would be a major splash of Gold Medals for U.S. boxers.

Ultimately, I think we won 10 of the 12 gold medals, or something like that.

I also got to cover some major characters in the process. Mike Tyson, for example, was eliminated in the box-off at Fort Worth, Texas, for the U.S. team by an ex-con named Henry Tillman. You may remember quite a bit about Tyson, but what do you remember about Tillman?

I was sent to cover that event, plus a similar "box-off" in Las Vegas.

In August of 1984, I covered 347 fights in the Olympics, all at the L.A. Sports Arena. And I haven't been in attendance at a prize fight since.

Covering the Olympics was spectacular, mostly because Southern California was so into the event. Major employers shut plants and offices, or gave employees a two-week holiday. Traffic flowed without gridlock, and L.A. celebrated in the world's eye. Although detailed to the boxing event, my pass allowed me to get into other venues, and I enjoyed a few sessions of track and field at the Coliseum.

But the way the Games were spread out all over Southern California, I was not able to go visit the volleyball (Long Beach) or some other sports I had an interest in. I was resigned to watching a lot of Olympics on television, just like everyone else.

The Copley papers rented a fraternity house on West Adams near the USC campus for its 20-man crew from outside the L.A. area. I spent time between the afternoon and evening sessions at the Sports Arena at this house. There was a cook who served meals to order. But I commuted back and forth to Redondo Beach on freeways that moved as they were designed to in the 1960s.

SKI TRAVEL: THE NATIONALS (1984)

Ski racing was as individual as any sport could be – until an advertising agency came up with a way to make recreational racing a team sport. And that turned out to be a great way to promote a product.

First, consider the demographic. Skiers were young, active, adventurous, and generally had enough disposable income to afford trips to far away mountain resorts.

And they were likely to consume an advertiser's product, especially if it fit their lifestyle.

That's why Grand Marnier liquor was a great fit for a sponsorship involving ski clubs and their recreational racers. We already had a thriving program at Mammoth Mountain, with ski clubs organized into leagues and racers divided into handicap groups so that every 20 or 25 racers would be a new class. And a new champion. And if you worked hard at it, you could move up through the ranks.

The handicap system was solid and the programs were thriving in the 1970s and '80s. The group was ripe for an ad agency to make it a viable campaign.

The idea: call it the Ski Club Challenge, design a format that encompassed all ages and both genders, and make the prizes worth pursuing. The Grand Marnier Ski Club Challenge was a hit from the start, and later continued on with another logical sponsor, Jeep.

For the Mammoth regional, one of six around the country, there were nearly 40 teams, with the winning club team receiving a trip to Colorado for the National Championship. Ski clubs put together teams based on age and gender, with three men and three women competing in age groups (21-29, 30-39 and 40-over). You got to throw out your slowest time, and the fastest five runs over a dual slalom course constituted your score.

Since ski club racers in So Cal tended to race for a lot of clubs (so we could race in all five leagues), there was competition for the teams and the spots. The best racers in each spot were sought after.

I was on the Beach Cities B team in 1984, a good group, but not a threat to win against the best teams in the state. In fact, our A team was the winner at Mammoth. But a week before the trip to Keystone, Colorado, and the nationals, our middle guy, Mike Seydor, blew out a knee and was headed for surgery. I was the choice on short notice (Saturday for a Monday departure).

I joined Sam Soule and Scott Peer, as well as Danielle Battut, Ellen Gaar and Diane Durant.

This was 1984, pre-9/11 regulations. Tickets were transferrable. So, I just took Seydor's paper ticket and joined the group.

For a brief moment or two, I was worried about being competitive enough, since Seydor was a notch above me in the race rankings. But when we got to Colorado and started our warmup runs, Scott Peer set us straight. We would not be competitive for the championship against some hard-core racers from the east. Scott knew, since he was our most hard-core racer and the only one in our group capable of winning his age group.

Scott called an impromptu meeting at the condo we were sharing, and everyone spread out the party favors they brought. Everyone but Sam and Danielle, who were not on the party bus. There was alcohol, marijuana, cocaine, and perhaps a few other flavors.

The way Scott saw it, we might not be in the running to win, but we could have the most fun. And Scott was an excellent leader. Although he was the fastest ski racer in So Cal, at the age of 27, he also had an innocent choir-boy look that was a wonderful disguise.

When Scott led us into the woods for a Team Meeting, between practice or race runs, who would suspect it was for nothing more than to pass around a joint? Our team meetings became legendary and we picked up a few followers, including a fast racer from New Hampshire who was either interested in our young female racer, our grass, or both.

As predicted early in the week, we finished 5th or 6th out of 6 teams. But we had a lot of fun. We also did well at the party, when our team drink finished second in the competition. The challenge was to make a drink that included Grand Marnier. I modified a vodka-based mix that got the judges' eyes. And we had a great time.

By week's end, Beach Cities was known as a great party team. The winning teams earned skis, boots, poles and bindings, plus logo bags. By the time you got down to our spot, the prize was lightweight travel duffle bags. Because it said "1984 National Championships," it became a favorite and I still have it to this day.

Memories of my only national championship competition: Finishing sixth of six men in the highly competitive 30-39 age group, almost winning the drink mixing competition, and participating in those legendary team meetings in the woods.

There was also the trip home. On a Saturday in ski season, Denver's old Stapleton airport was a zoo. Tens of thousands of folks came and went through the airport on Saturdays, lugging ski gear and other bags. When the bus from Keystone dropped us off, there was chaos, and nobody to help with our luggage.

Being the most experienced traveler in the group, I sought out a sky-cap and quickly impressed him with my knowledge of American Presidents and other legends, most notably Ben Franklin. A couple of Franklins got his attention and he wrangled the gear for we six into the line.

There were other ski trips and specifically ones for our annual races. We alternated between Tahoe and Mammoth and often rented houses or condos for a group to enjoy the extended weekend. I don't so much remember the championships as the near misses, and the camaraderie.

For the most part, I took my ski racing seriously – at least between the starting and finish lines. After that, the results spoke for themselves.

One year when Mammoth hosted the NASJA annual meeting, we were bused to June Mountain for our ski race. I brought along my (long) giant slalom skis, which were probably 215 centimeters. After finishing second in the serious race, a disappointment, I was told there would be a "fun" race in a team format.

I was so not looking for fun, I started asking various Race Department employees who might be driving back to Mammoth early. They were stuck at June, and so was I.

When I found out the format for the "fun" race, I was even less thrilled. I was going to be part of a relay that carried a cake down the mountain, decorating it at one stop. My well-tuned 215-cm racing skis were wasted in this silliness. Yet our team managed to win.

After the announcement at the banquet, I realized that the "silly" race had produced the largest prize of my ski racing career: An all-expense paid trip for two to Quebec for three days of skiing at Mont-Sainte-Anne, airfare included. Nancy and I enjoyed our trip, and nine months later, we welcomed Randy to the world.

So much for being serious about ski racing.

HE MARRIED UP: NANCY (1985)

In the four years since breaking up with Patt Robinson in 1981, and moving into the condo on Prospect, I had pretty much reconciled myself to a life of short-term relationships, events that filled the needs of the moment but held little chance for being lasting or meaningful.

In short, I was single at a time when being single was very conducive to my lifestyle. Finding companionship, or more, was easy in the 1970s and early 1980s.

When Lorraine and I divorced in the fall of 1974, I started hanging out with a group of mostly teachers that I met at the beach playing volleyball.

Florence (Flossie) Duff was a middle school math teacher in Palos Verdes who came from Pennsylvania. She was athletic, and she loved sports. We began playing as volleyball partners, and then later dated for most of three years. But that's dated with an asterisk, since unbeknownst to the rest of our crowd, Flossie had a secret. She was also in love with a married man, who eventually left his wife and they got married while living in Mammoth years later.

Ours was not a monogamous relationship, because of her secret lover. We were together a lot, but I was free to entertain other options, which fit my lifestyle perfectly in those days. The only problem was that friends might occasionally feel the need to share with Flossie when they saw another car parked behind mine.

Flossie and I were partners in the condo in Mammoth, and when I decided I needed to get back into home ownership in the South Bay, she was a partner.

That condo, on Vanderbilt Lane in North Redondo, was where I met and fell in love with Patt Robinson. That relationship lasted about three years, and progressed to the point where invitations were printed and plans were being made for a wedding.

But the difficulty of living with her then 13- or 14-year-old daughter, and our diverging interests, made it clear we were incompatible.

After the relationship with Patt blew up, I was no longer looking for a lifelong companion, if I ever was. When we split up, my real estate friend, Sharon Blanks, found a way for me to move into a newly built condo, for basically nothing down, with her as my silent partner. That was 1981, when I moved into the condo at 220 South Prospect, in Redondo Beach.

The condo worked perfectly for a lifestyle that I embraced in those days.

The women who rotated through that condo were all pleasant, fun to be around, and most had no more interest in anything lasting than I did. There might have been one or two that saw further into the future than Saturday, but once their intentions became apparent, I quickly quashed those ideas.

There was one misunderstood relationship in 1982, the NFL Strike year, when I had knee surgery and spent six weeks in a full-leg cast. A ski club friend became a regular during my difficult days. But when the cast came off around November, and I realized she was making plans for Thanksgiving and Christmas with her family, we needed to have a conversation. That was more long-term than I was planning.

Was I happy with the lifestyle? Was I content? Hard to say in the distant rear-view mirror of 2020. But it was what I had. I wasn't looking for a wife. Most of what I wanted and needed could be acquired on a short-term basis.

After three years spending my summers in Santa Rosa covering the Raiders' training camp, things were about to change. The team had decided it was more practical to spend their summer six weeks closer to their year-round home, now in El Segundo. Santa Rosa was a great adventure for me and I loved being on the road. But a training camp in Oxnard had its own version of attraction.

It was about a month before the move to Oxnard when I was winding down my summer activities as a slightly better than average beach volleyball player. Our ski clubs participated in four summer tournaments on the courts south of the pier in Manhattan Beach, and these were major days of athletics and beer. Not necessarily in that order.

I was good enough to win regularly in doubles during the week, and good enough to be on the ski club's No. 2 volleyball team for the 6-man tournaments. It was one of these Sundays when my life changed.

After six or eight hours of volleyball, I was tired, and there was sand in places on my body that I would prefer not to mention. My friend Nick Duvalley, then a captain with L.A. County Fire Department and later a Battalion Chief, was renting part of a big house on the Strand near the courts in Manhattan Beach. So South Bay Ski Club would hold its after-volleyball party at Nick's place. This was just another opportunity to drink beer, eat a little, commiserate or brag about the day's volleyball, and wind down

I was working on a beer, or six, when I watched some sweet young thing – younger than me, clearly new to the scene – trying to talk about skiing with one of the veteran males in the group. I was not really interested, until I got tired of this terminal intermediate skier trying to impress the sweet young thing with his skiing knowledge.

I will never forget this snippet of conversation:

Sweet Young Thing: "What's the weather like when you have powder snow?"

Old Intermediate Guy: "Oh, it's sunny and warm …."

Halt! Stop! Wait a minute! I was just not going to allow this guy – his name was Fidel – to bullshit the sweet young thing. Everybody knows that the conditions that lead to great powder skiing include very cold and dry weather. Not warm days – which contribute to wet sloppy snow.

I interrupted and told Fidel to knock off the bullshit. I introduced myself to Sweet Young Thing, and pulled her away from Fidel. We talked a bit, and some sort of magic dust must have appeared, because I realized I was not ready to meet somebody looking as bedraggled as I did. … I excused myself for a moment – introducing Sweet Young Thing to somebody I knew could entertain her for 20 minutes – and found Nick's shower and borrowed some clean shorts and a t-shirt.

When I reappeared, refreshed and showered, Nancy and I started talking a little more seriously. Turns out she had just moved to the South Bay after getting her first job as a Physical Therapist, and the woman who cut her hair invited her to the ski club after-volleyball party as a way to meet people.

Diverging dramatically from the way I had fulfilled my needs in recent years, something told me to move slowly – we talked some more, then I invited her to my place for a jacuzzi. And instead of a full-court press for instant gratification, it was more about conversation and getting to know you.

We made a date for the next night, or maybe it was Tuesday, and we continued getting to know one another. Quite a departure for me, but the results are worth noting. A week or so later, I wanted to go up to Oxnard to check out the hotel where I would be spending the next six weeks, and Nancy joined me. I commuted back and forth to the South Bay throughout training camp, and before long, we realized she should move in.

On June 14, 1987, we were married, and this year, we celebrated our 33rd wedding anniversary.

Thanks to Fidel, who I have not seen in 30 years, for bullshitting the Sweet Young Thing, who I quickly realized was somebody worth spending more than a little time with.

A few years later, I made the decision to give up alcohol – the other major decision in my life – and our marriage flourished. We lived an active life and traveled often, with Nancy becoming a competent advanced skier. She also became part of the volleyball group, learning another sport.

Randy arrived at the end of 1990, and Allie followed in 1996. We moved to our house on Onrado Street in Torrance on July 4, 1996 – three months after Allie was born – and continue to grow our relationship.

For a guy who didn't know whether marriage was ever going to happen again in his life, I was the luckiest guy around. Nancy was a strong force in every way, with a great profession as a physical therapist. I was very fortunate to marry into a great family and treasure the relationships with all of them.

In 1996, when South Bay Ski Club named me Member of the Year, friend John Funtsch made a great point out of what a difference Nancy had made in my life. I couldn't agree more.

Although this book is a recollection of a lot of events spanning many decades, the positive things that have marked my life in the last 30 years should be traced directly to Nancy. In the vernacular of the 1980s, it's fair to say I definitely married up

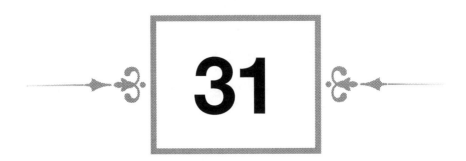

ON THE ROAD: EL PASO (1987)

In the late spring of 1987, Nancy was working hard to finish the details on our June 14 wedding. I was working to stay out of the office since it was the offseason for NFL writers.

After a couple of hours on the desk in the morning helping put out our afternoon edition, I would often adjourn to the Redondo Beach public library to do research on a major piece on unions in sports. How dated is doing research at a library?

Our assistant sports editor knew where to find me, and had the librarian page me for a phone call – no cell phones in 1987 – and it was one of those remarkable calls.

A local athlete playing basketball at UTEP (Texas El Paso) had passed away from an overdose of cocaine. And the *Breeze* budget was robust enough that we should go investigate. Could I get on a plane later that afternoon?

I flew to Denver, then El Paso, and was in a suite at the El Paso Westin that night. By the next day, I was visiting the school and the basketball coach. Not surprisingly, no one suspected that Jeep Jackson, the player who followed his skills from Gardena to a major college team, was using illegal drugs.

This was a time when drug abuse was just becoming widespread among athletes. An NBA first-round draft choice, Len Bias from Maryland, had recently overdosed on cocaine. Some were calling the NBA the National

Cocaine League. But it was still a surprise when a college athlete dies from substance abuse.

My mandate was to investigate the death, the drug scene in El Paso, and to give the *Breeze* lively on-site coverage that no other Southern California newspaper might have. In addition to campus sources, I also connected with the police chief and the district attorney.

That got me through a couple of in-depth stories, but then I knew it was time to start digging. This was El Paso before the Cartel Drug Wars, back when passage across the border between El Paso and Juarez was free and easy.

In trying to create sources besides the obvious ones, I spent time in campus hangouts and tried to find out where a 21-year-old college junior with minimal money might obtain cocaine.

I was directed to the Mexican town of Ciudad Juarez. Again, this was before Juarez became the murder capital of North America. It was suggested I not take my rental car across the border, but other than that, there were no worries about working the Mexican side of the border. My self-assigned mission, find out how Jeep Jackson was able to score cheap cocaine in Juarez.

One of Jackson's friends suggested I visit the store-front dentists in Juarez. I did, feigning a toothache, and asked for pain medication. For about $5, I got a cursory examination and a prescription for pain medication. But I did not score a script for La Coca. After four or five dentists had confirmed that I had lousy teeth, and were willing to fill a cheap prescription for pain medication, I got the point. In each case, I asked for La Coca, and in each case, I was turned down.

Jackson may have gotten his cocaine from a Juarez dentist, but I was not as successful. Granted, I was nearly 20 years older and maybe did not fit the bill for a drug-using college student.

I worked a few other angles, tried to get close to those who knew Jeep Jackson off the basketball court, and found that he was a risk-taker willing to do what it took to succeed in basketball. The school held a memorial ceremony, and his number was retired by the team, but nobody was able to find out how he acquired his cocaine.

After about a week, and a number of investigative pieces, I was running out of angles. I was also tiring of living on the road and trying to score cocaine.

I concluded that from the perspective of a college athlete – who may have been receiving cash handouts from alumni – it was probably pretty easy to acquire cocaine and marijuana. But I was not able to replicate the purchase in the storefront dental shops in Juarez.

I made it through a second weekend, and spent a little more time in Juarez, but the story ideas were running dry. It was time to pull the plug and head home. I'm not sure what the *Breeze* editors expected from this adventure in journalism, but by all accounts, they were happy. The *Breeze* got a series of stories about the premature death of a local sports hero, but there was no Pulitzer based on my investigative reporting. I did a solid job, but only confirmed what many knew to be true. Sports and drugs were a pretty common marriage in the 1980s.

MY BIGGEST DECISION (1994)

Every aspect of my life had involved alcohol, from perhaps age 16 on. What to drink, where to buy it, how much to drink, how to hide my drinking, etc. In short, it was such an integral part of my life that I could not image a life without it.

I wasn't a stumbling around, falling-down drunk. I was mostly functioning pretty well, although there were a few moments when that was not the case. There had been a couple of arrests for driving under the influence, although in the mood of the times – pre-Mothers Against Drunk Driving – one was reduced to what they euphemistically called a "wet reckless."

One became a conviction although the only jail time was a couple of hours to dry out. When daughter Allie heard parts of another story, which included the fact I had been arrested in 1981, she demanded to know details and why she'd never heard about it. Well, maybe because it happened 15 years before you were born, and did you really have a "need to know?"

Probably the more important and ongoing aspect of that arrest (which was in Fullerton), was that it did nothing to change my habits or my lifestyle.

I still drank often and regularly. Every day, in short. I still bought Scotch by the large container (what used to be a half-gallon and was later reduced to 1.75 liters). And I never left myself in a position to run out. There was also beer, wine, vodka, gin and tequila, depending on the circumstances, of course. But Scotch was the beverage I turned to on a nightly basis.

I may have been fooling others – there could be dissenting opinions on this – but I certainly was not fooling myself. I knew I drank a lot, and that it was too much a part of my life. But I was not talking about it to anyone. That was a characteristic I later had to deal with in group therapy, but I was not someone who shared.

To her credit, Nancy was never a nagger. She coped with my drinking, much as I did. She was aware, but we did not have arguments over it. Credit Nancy for knowing that would not have been a successful approach. We did have a couple of conversations in the last year of my drinking life, and I was coming around to some realities. Just wasn't there yet.

Through our connection with the Raiders, I started seeing Dr. Rob Huizenga as my GP doctor. He was the team's internist and traveled with the Raiders. He dealt with medical issues for players, coaches and staff on the road, and helped the writers out on occasion. What kind of medical issue might a traveling sports team have to deal with? Think social ailments, among others.

Early one morning, I visited his offices near Cedars-Sinai Medical Center in Hollywood for an executive physical. Rob was about my age and had been an athlete in crew and lacrosse as an undergraduate at Michigan before medical school. His physical was intense and all-encompassing. I went back a week later to discuss the results of the blood test.

Dr. Huizenga minced no words. "Bob, you're killing yourself. And looking at your liver tests, you're going to die, sooner rather than later."

Strong words from someone I deeply respected. He had severed ties with the Raiders after writing a book condemning the medical care football players and others got because it was all about getting athletes back on the field, rather than healing them.

He was a man of principle who was willing to give up a lucrative practice for something he believed in.

He wasn't going to sugar-coat things for me.

The trip home that day was the beginning of the process for the most important decision I would ever make. I knew the end result, the answer, but I did not understand the process, or how to get there.

Many celebrities had gone to the Betty Ford Center in Rancho Mirage for addiction therapy. It was the famous 28-day miracle cure. I figured they would send me to "the tank" for a month and I'd come out cured. I had no idea what that meant. But I wanted to get cured.

Then, as now, the insurance carriers made the most meaningful decisions on health-care. They sent me to a psychiatrist, who nixed the expensive, month-long inpatient treatment in favor of a hospital-based intensive program. After a couple of weeks of working through the health-care process, and my own personal process, I was ready to take the most important steps of my life.

If this sounds melodramatic, understand that I could not remember the last day when I had not had a drink – perhaps a couple of years back when I'd had knee surgery? Also, I believed that much of my professional self-confidence came from drinking.

Nancy knew it was the only way she and our 3-year-old son were going to have me around, and was encouraging. We agreed to a limited release of information within the family, at first. And while I shared with new sports editor Greg Gibson, I was not telling my friends or sources in sports. Maybe I wanted a path back if things did not work out. Maybe I was hedging my bet in case I failed.

From the beginning, I realized sobriety was a full-time job, starting with the three days I had to spend at a group home in Hawthorne where they could monitor my detoxification. There were a couple of drugs involved, but the biggest factor was this was the beginning of a commitment. I was an alcoholic and it was time to admit it to the world.

One takeaway from the group home – you bring almost nothing, including money, to the residence. I did not remember shampoo, and when we walked to a nearby convenience store, I had to borrow two bucks to buy shampoo. The counselor was used to dealing with alcoholics and was pretty sure she'd never see those two bucks again. I convinced her, and when I was released, I made it a point of getting the money back to her. Maybe that was one of my first steps.

The program was at Torrance Memorial Hospital, and we met in various groups for most of the day for about two weeks. We attended regular group sessions, including the Alcoholics Anonymous format, and were encouraged to share as we became comfortable.

It took me a while to share, since I had to work through a resentment about needing to be there. What did I resent? Maybe that I had a weakness, that I couldn't cure on my own. We went to AA meetings with the group during the day, and also had to attend five or seven others each week. The daily sessions lasted several weeks.

After we were equipped with the tools that would give us a chance at sobriety, we were eased back into our regular lives. We did some bonding among our fellow addicts, and started attending AA meetings together to support one another.

While the whole process is a bit of a blur, I remember a few key moments. One night early on, I stopped at a liquor store on the way to an AA meeting and bought one of those little canned mixed drinks that I had become accustomed to over the years. I was going to drink it before the AA meeting. Then I got a grip on myself, and wondered why I was going through this process if I was going to screw it up after my first two weeks of sobriety since Navy boot camp.

I threw the canned drink away and didn't tell a soul how close I had come to screwing things up. Later, I realized that was a perfect item for sharing in the group meetings.

Since Randy was about 3 at the time, I remember the story of a fellow addict, about how he trained his 4-year-old son to bring him beers. That was another benchmark which helped solidify my commitment.

I was at the point where I could go back to work after about three weeks or a month. And while I had told Greg Gibson, I had not told my other co-workers on the sports staff. I called up Mike Waldner, the former sports editor, and a friend, and Dan McLean, my oldest friend on the staff. And I vowed that I was not going to be touchy about the subject.

There were also some major friends who had to know. John Funtsch, John Catozzi, Jim Benz, and a few others. They had been with me through years of heavy drinking, so none was surprised.

One of my other commitments came on the weekend after my first week of classes. I put all of the alcohol bottles from our condo into a couple of boxes and took them over to Jim Benz's house for "safe-keeping." I think I told him that if I didn't ask for them back in a month, or some such time, they were his to keep. Twenty-five years later, we have never talked about those bottles of booze.

There were so many firsts to work through in my path to sobriety, not to mention just spending a night without the self-anesthetizing of booze.

When I got on a plane to fly to the Raiders' first preseason game, in Pittsburgh in August, I realized this was the first time I had been on a plane without a few warmup drinks in more than 20 years. When the flight attendant offered me a beverage, I asked for mineral water. And I sipped the bubbly water like it was a fine Scotch.

There were also the first deadline-write stories after games, learning I could cope without a cocktail.

That winter, I went on a ski trip to Whistler/Blackcomb, B.C., and several friends were there to help. I learned to find the Non-Alcoholic beer the Canadians call Point-Five (for its alcoholic content). That helped during the social events.

Part of the positive of giving up thousands of dead calories a day was the weight loss. I dropped more than 40 pounds and settled in at about 155. Combined with a regular daily visit to the gym, I was in great shape. And when we had our ski club race as part of the Whistler trip, I was the fastest racer in the group of nearly 150 skiers.

That presented another dilemma. We were going to an end-of-trip banquet, and the hall where we were going to be did not have the NA beers. I was worried since I had never been to a banquet without pre-dinner cocktails. But I had good friends on that trip. Jim Benz was always supportive, but it was Mike Sremba and Liz Morski that got me through the banquet.

After our waitress confirmed they could not serve NA beer when they were bringing around wine and cocktails, Liz entertained me while Mike left the banquet hall and walked a couple of blocks to a liquor store and bought me four NA beers. When he returned, I was thrilled. Those NA beers were an important step for me on the path to recovery. They helped me get up and receive the award for fastest racer. And I walked back to our condo with Mike and Liz later that night feeling even more confident.

Every time some new event came up, I had to deal with a first time without alcohol. But they got easier.

I also attended AA meetings with conviction. I received the coveted 30, 60 and 90-day medals to mark sobriety. I still believe the 30-day pin I earned was the best trophy I've ever received. I went to meetings all over the South Bay and at all times of day and night. When I went on the road, I learned how to find meetings and attend in several cities where I was visiting for a football game.

I even found and attended the meetings in Mammoth – where I had supported the bar industry for 20 plus years. Now, when Nancy and I go on cruises, we notice on the daily agenda where the Friends of Bill are meeting. This is the socially reference to the AA meetings.

I stopped attending meetings on a regular basis sometime in my second year of sobriety. Not that I felt I was strong enough to do it on my own, since that is a critical blunder for most alcoholics, but I knew I was finding other ways to avoid my personal downfalls.

As I write this now, I am approaching 26 years of sobriety. I am becoming somewhat of a connoisseur of NA beers, and often have one or two a night before dinner. Back in my drinking days, I would never have had one or two of anything.

And my liver tests, which triggered Rob Huizenga's "you're killing yourself" plea, are outstanding. That is one incredibly regenerative organ.

MY ATHLETIC KIDS (2000-2018)

Randy and Allie both got major benefits out of sports. And I was with them all the way, also benefitting while living vicariously through them.

Randy's early sports life was a blur of rec leagues and AYSO soccer, and minimal success or pleasure. But something or someone motivated him about the time he was finishing middle school, and suddenly he was a workout maniac who wanted to play football.

I think the biggest shock I ever received regarding Randy and sports was that summer between 8th and 9th grades. We were on a driving trip to Northern California, with the main attraction being a river-rafting trip. Along the way, we worked our way through the Gold Rush Era towns of California, en route to Lake Tahoe.

At one of those older towns, we were walking around, and Randy asked if we had a little time. He wanted to run the steps – maybe 150 of them – of the 1860s courthouse. As we watched in wonder, he attacked the steps, He had clearly learned much from the early-summer football camp, and he was working to stay in shape.

He went on to play four years of football at Torrance High School, as an offensive tackle. He wasn't gifted with the speed, or the ball skills, or the other aspects of stardom, but he had the tenacity and the knowledge of teamwork that made him a quality offensive lineman.

He loved the sport, and part of being a team, and it gave me a chance to share some of his experiences.

I was able to volunteer all four years. When he was on the freshman team, I started out keeping stats for Coach Bob Zuliani, then shifted to handling the coach's portable camera to create game films.

During one game, at Lawndale – where I would later work – I was bored with the Torrance offense. When the team went off the field at halftime, I filmed the Tartar cheerleaders and their routines. Zuliani didn't get a chance to pre-screen the movies before showing them to the players, so there was apparently a lot of laughter when the half-time show came on the screen. The coach may have also questioned my motives. But he never said anything to me.

The next year, when Randy was playing JV (and suiting up for varsity), I was back to doing statistics.

And for Randy's final two years on varsity, I was the statistician. One of those years, Torrance won the Pioneer League championship and advanced to the CIF Playoffs. It was an exciting time to be around Tartar football.

I was part of the game-day crew of volunteers, which included a half-dozen long-time friends of the Coach Rock Hollis. I got to hang around the coaches before games, and learned about the high school version of the sport I had loved for nearly 20 years at the NFL level.

Friday Night Lights later became a major motion picture, and a TV series, highlighting the life of a high school coach and his athletes. It was a family affair for the Cox Family, too. Randy was the player, and I was keeping stats, while Nancy was selling programs in the stands, and Allie was on the sidelines as a ball girl, flipping the footballs to the officiating crew.

On Senior Night, Randy was one of the captains and we all posed for a great family picture. We all shared Randy's love and appreciation for the game. And it gave Randy and me something to talk about for the rest of our lives.

Allie's early sports career was similarly lackluster since soccer mattered little to her, and her appearance on a Torrance rec league softball team was mostly something I had ignored.

When it came time to take her to tryouts for her first season at Torrance Girls Softball League, we had played catch a couple of times, and I had pitched some batting practice for her, but neither of us knew the major impact the sport would have on our lives.

On that day, she was about to turn 7 years old, and I had not given much thought to my daughter, the athlete. During the tryouts, one of the adults coordinating things said the league was looking for coaches. Not sure what the magic was, or how it struck us both, but Allie said, "would you?" and I agreed, and both of our lives were forever changed.

Like everything else in my life, I threw myself into coaching girls' softball. I read books on coaching softball, I attended clinics, I asked advice, and I watched how other dads handled things.

By the end of our first season, I was on the league's board of directors as an age group coordinator. At the end of that first season, I was asked to coach a second all-star team in three tournaments to get girls more experience. Allie didn't feel strongly enough about softball that summer to be on that team, so I learned while coaching 12 girls with no family ties.

My claim to fame from that first summer all-star team, oft cited at board meetings years later: Of the 12 girls on that team, 11 continued to play softball through at least age 12. The one who didn't was committed to soccer, where she was a major star.

By the next season, my enthusiasm for softball, and Allie's, started to merge, I was committed to being the best coach possible, and was hoping she would find that contagious. Like many coach's kids, she became a pitcher. That meant we spent a lot of time together, practicing her craft.

We threw at least three days every week in season, in addition to practicing with the team, and paid sessions with her official pitching coach, as well as batting lessons. Softball became a way of life for us.

That doesn't mean it always went smoothly. There were a lot of days when pitching wasn't high on Allie's list of things to do, and I had to find a way to coax or cajole her into the sessions. I may have used every trick in my book, including referencing the successes of girls a year or two older.

When she connected with Cindy Cherness in Vet School in their 20s, she regaled her friend with stories of how I would tell her, "Cindy Cherness is out throwing 100 pitches right now," in hopes of getting her to the practice field.

I wound up as manager or head coach of four of the next five all-star teams, and Allie was a player on all of them. I was an assistant coach on the other team, because I had just taken on a major new job at LAUSD and chose to be an assistant coach rather than a head coach during the regular season.

In softball, making the all-star team is almost a guarantee of stepping up your skill level. After playing a regular season with your assigned team, you and your elite teammates play in five or six tournaments in the summer, against similarly higher-level opposition. You travel around Southern California, and often spend weekends at hotels near the tournament site. In short, you play an entire second season, and your improvement is noticeable.

By Allie's last two years at TGSL, ages 11 and 12, she was one of the best players in the league, and my knowledge of the sport and its intricacies had increased exponentially.

As Allie progressed through the ranks, I spent more and more time studying the career paths of girls who had succeeded, moving from Rec Ball at TGSL, to Travel Ball, and into high school sports. The peak of the pyramid continues to get smaller as girls move up, and only a few get to keep playing their sport in college.

When it was time to make the leap to Travel Ball, for her age 13 season, I was ready to be part of the process, too. I was asked to form a 14-and-under team for the successful Mizuno Pride organization. Instead of coaching the girls you are assigned, as in Rec Ball, in Travel Ball you can recruit and find the best talent available.

In Rec Ball you might have four girls who could play, four who could not, and four who were in the middle and could go either way. In Travel Ball, you held tryouts and players from all over So Cal attended, looking to be on the best team where they could still get playing time.

I wound up coaching three years with the Pride organization, two as head coach and a third as manager while importing a female coach who had been a collegiate player. Tiffany Johnson had come onto my radar when she applied for a teaching job at Centinela Valley. She had played at Arkansas and Portland State.

When she came out to help coach our Pride girls, I made it a point of asking her not to take it easy on Allie. Tiffany took that as a mandate to be harder on Allie than on anyone else and it created some tough times. Allie learned more from Tiffany, and later Eddie Davis, than she did when I was coaching. Part of it was learning to deal with difficult situations. Not playing, making mistakes, getting chewed out.

Years later, when things went wrong and she faced the wrath of a college coach, she was able to handle it. To this day, she does not speak kindly of Tiffany, but she does have a lot of respect for Eddie. And she acknowledges that she was able to handle adversity in college because of what she learned from them.

There was also a stretch during her Pride years when I was battling cancer, and I was a mere shadow of my former self. I was on the bench, keeping the scorebook, but not much else.

After her year under Eddie Davis, the Pride organization decided to fold its tent, which was good timing for us. Allie was ready to look around. Frankie Flores of the Diamond Girls invited her to a tryout, and things blossomed from that point on. She was reunited with McCall James, the pitcher from El Segundo who I recruited for the first Pride team. And she thrived in a positive atmosphere. Frankie and wife Lorraine Flores continue to run one of the most successful travel organizations.

I learned a lot about pitch calling from Frankie – he loved to set up batters for Allie's slow curve and then get them on that pitch for the strikeout.

I was also able to bring some things from the Pride to the Diamond Girls, such as the sponsorship agreement with Mizuno, and a relationship that got us into the prestigious Champion's Cup tournament.

During this time, and while Allie was playing softball and volleyball in high school, we were looking at options for her future college home. We attended a lot of camps, where coaches will time, measure and film players.

And we started visiting colleges. I wanted Allie to have a good sense of what she wanted in a school when the time came.

Much like we had given Lisa a tour of California universities back in the 1980s, and we had also taken Randy on college tours, we started to set up Allie with a map of her college options, almost all of them included visits with the softball coach.

My most vivid memory was of our first trip to Oregon, where we started at Southern Oregon University. Allie and I were sitting in the cramped office of the coach, who was talking about her program, then started asking questions. Allie was intimidated, and stumbled to respond. I knew the answers, but also knew the coach didn't want to hear from me, so my mouth was taped.

Allie was a quick learner. And a few visits later, she was handling the coach's questions with ease, and had her own set of questions. After that summer visit, she was invited to Southern Oregon for a campus visit in the fall, and she made her first-ever trip entirely on her own. I felt confident I had showed her how to get around airports, and the rest of the world, but she was still only 15.

By the next summer, when she and Nancy made an eastern trip to visit Wheaton College, she knew what she wanted and how to ask about it. She was poised and confident. And when the two coaches at Wheaton, Rachael Powers for softball and Craig LeTourneau for volleyball, decided they wanted her, I was thrilled.

Wheaton played Division 3, rather than the highest level of Division 1 (UCLA, etc.) which meant she could play two sports. They also did not offer Athletic Scholarships, but offered Merit Awards based on factors of their choosing. Allie was awarded $15,000 per year for her four years. That and Nancy's inheritance from her father helped us afford the $60,000 annual cost.

Softball and volleyball helped Allie gain poise and confidence, and also gave her the inner strength to deal with adversity. She majored in biochemistry while playing two sports.

One of my proudest moments, among many, was that she still wanted me to catch her in practice sessions the winter before her senior year. I had battled cancer and lost a lot of strength and reaction time, but I was able to stay with her to the end of her pitching career. Granted, I had started to wear my umpiring facemask and shin guards by then, but I was able to catch this collegiate pitcher. Her ability to bounce a curve or a drop right behind the plate made her a successful pitcher, but also a challenge to catch.

It was another of the many bonding moments we shared in the sport.

After football, Randy threw himself into skiing, and worked as a ski instructor through college and for a couple of years afterwards. He and I had made a lot of ski trips during his teenage years.

Allie did not get as much time on the ski hill as her brother, but her competitive urge pushed her to catch up. When Nancy and I were able to take both kids (plus Randy's wife, Sylvie, and daughter Geneva) to Utah for skiing in February 2020, it was great to see how talented my two athletic kids were on the ski slopes.

STARTING OVER AT THE
AGE OF 50 (1998)

My once perfect life as a newspaperman started changing in 1995 when both the Raiders and Rams – our two NFL teams – decided to move away for better stadium options.

That was probably the symptom rather than the cause of the problem, but it helped crystalize my thinking on my life's work, among other things.

With football gone from my workaday life, and not coincidentally, with a new sports editor who was determined to prove his strength by bringing down the top dog, things were not looking good. I had a job, and could probably spend another 15 years doing it. But it wasn't the job I loved.

Mike Waldner had served double duty as sports editor, and columnist for many years. As the paper was growing, he was given the choice of being sports editor, or being a columnist. He made what many of us on staff thought was the wrong choice. Instead of being a great sports editor, he decided to become a ordinary columnist. It was the right choice for him, but tough on the staff. That opened the door for a new sports editor from the outside, something that hadn't happened at the *Breeze* in decades.

First time out, they made a great choice. Greg Gibson was a Long Beach product who had gone north to Tacoma, Wash., to establish himself as a great sports editor. But he wanted to return to So Cal. The *Breeze* editors even paid $10,000 to move him back, an unheard-of commitment from a notoriously frugal management team.

Gibson was widely hailed and instantly started beefing things up at the *Breeze*. Three months in, he was faced with the challenge of my decision to enter rehab for my alcohol problem. Not surprisingly, he handled that professionally.

Unfortunately for the *Breeze*, his renown was widespread, and *The Register* in Orange County saw him as a second in command with an eye to the top spot. And they offered to reimburse the *Breeze* for that $10k moving allowance. Gibson left after about six months.

While their first choice was excellent, the managers stubbed their toes second time around. A guy named Robert Whitley fancied himself as a bon vivant, wine expert, college basketball expert, and editor for hire. He had been living on a boat in San Diego Harbor, writing a freelance wine column, and filling vacation relief editor jobs at the flagship San Diego *Union*.

His view of the *Breeze* was of a poor relative to the *Union* that needed fixing. First fix was to let everyone know he was top dog. He accomplished that by humbling the veteran staff. Leadership by derogatory comment was the new standard.

He also had a bad habit of being an asshole. He found ways to humiliate everyone with his daily critiques. No one was immune, but some of us were more regular customers. The only good thing was that he would work for a few days at a time, then return to San Diego for a few days. And he lost interest quickly, so his time away grew longer.

I went from being a nationally known football writer to being the guy who edited the horse racing pages and the editions of our sport sections that went to outlying communities like San Pedro and Santa Monica.

It was desk work, accomplished on a 3 p.m. to midnight shift, and neither challenging nor satisfying. About the only good thing was I could go home for dinner.

Nancy and I had moved into a wonderful house in Torrance Gardens on July 4th weekend, 1996, with our 5½-year-old son Randy and 3-month-old daughter, Allie. The new house was an easy walk to Fern Elementary School, where Randy would start kindergarten in the fall.

While my work life became just a 3 p.m.-to-midnight job, my daytime hours were quickly tuned to getting Randy to Fern and picking him up in the afternoon. I would drop him off at day care in the afternoon and Nancy would pick him up when she got off work.

But Fern Elementary was quickly drawing me in. I started by volunteering one day a week in the library, helping volunteer librarian Darlene Crider. Then I started spending a few hours in Randy's classroom, assisting teacher Lois LaForest. Randy was in a K-1 combo class, and as a kindergartener, he benefited by the teacher's work with the 1st graders.

Then I got word that the volunteer who was putting on noon-league soccer and football was moving on. And I added that to my routine. I was spending 5 days a week as a volunteer at Fern, and loving it. Organizing the sports programs was a treat for me. And I kept noticing that the teachers seemed to enjoy coming to work.

I started exploring what it would take to become a teacher.

It started with finishing that long-neglected degree. During my various stints in school, I'd amassed more than enough units for a bachelor's degree, but they were not concentrated in one area. So, I made an appointment with a counselor at Cal State Dominguez Hills, my last attended school, and we figured out that the fastest path to a degree was in History. The school no longer offered American Studies (my last major), and I was further away in English, and I already had a minor in Sociology. I needed seven classes, which I could easily amass in three semesters. Between working nights at the Breeze, volunteering at Fern and attending CSUDH, I was a busy fellow from spring 1997 through spring of 1998, covering three semesters.

I also learned that after achieving the BA, I would need to get a teaching credential. That required passing a couple of tests and getting accepted into a credential program. I studied for the tests with a fervor I had rarely exhibited elsewhere in life. First there was the multiple subject assessment exam, which would get me into the District Intern program – a free credential program run by the giant Los Angeles Unified School District. Elementary teachers are expected to know a little about a lot of subjects, 10 to be exact.

My studies for the MSAT were my first realization of what I needed to do. I worked hard on the subjects I knew best, figuring to maximize those points. I did not spend a lot of time on science – a weak spot then and now – knowing I had too much to learn to realistically score well in that area.

When I got to the test site, I heard a lot of teachers currently working on emergency credentials talking about this being their fourth or fifth try taking the test. I vowed that I would only need a maximum of two tries – if I fell short the first time, I would at least know the enemy and with a good scouting report, I'd pass by the second try.

Turns out I needed only one try. All of that energy that had previously gone into my writing job, or maybe my alcoholism, was focused into preparing for the MSAT. Passing that opened doors for me.

Another mandatory test was the California Basic Skills Test, or CBEST. While the MSAT was a monster, CBEST was a drivers license exam. Years later, when I hear about teachers not being able to pass this, I keep thinking that making it easier would be a huge mistake. This was and is the easy test.

All of which got me an interview with LAUSD and a chance to begin teaching as a District Intern – full salary while attending classes one night a week for two years for free and earning my Multiple Subjects Credential.

Good things kept happening as I moved further and further into education. After my interview with LAUSD and pending my acceptance into the District Intern program, I was given permission to find a teaching job. I attacked this like everything else in my suddenly wide-open future. I got a list of LAUSD schools in the South Bay / Harbor area and started sending out resumes and cover letters.

LAUSD was and is the second largest school district in the country and spreads out over an area as large as some small states. Its closest elementary schools weren't far from Torrance.

My first interview was at a school called Caroldale Learning Community (part of a trend towards the LEARN approach to education that was in vogue at the time). I learned that Caroldale was not only an elementary school (K-5th grade), but also had a small middle school (grades 6th through 8th) on the same campus in Carson. It was only about four miles from our home in Torrance.

While I was hardly your typical new teacher (young, just out of school), I must have said a few of the right things in my interview. Maybe my two years as a volunteer at Fern helped. Maybe my rush back to education to get that long-neglected degree. Who knows what the hiring committee liked? It was a group of a half dozen teachers led by the assistant principal, Dennis Ebel. I never met the principal until I was on campus to start work.

Ebel might have been my major benefactor. A former Catholic priest, he came to education as a second career. He was also an all-but-out-of-the-closet gay man.

After the interview, he called to offer me the job. Emboldened by my first success, I asked for a few days to conclude other interviews at schools in the area. None of them offered a job and I accepted Caroldale's offer to teach a 4/5 (4th and 5th grade) combo class, starting in Fall 1998.

This was the spring of 1998, and I had not officially received my BA yet – although it was in the works – and other great things were happening.

That same spring, the newspaper world started realizing it was losing business (ads, plus circulation) to the internet. While TV news couldn't kill us in the 1970s and 1980s, the Internet was kicking our butt. *The Breeze* and Copley Newspapers offered the first of what would become an ongoing series of buyouts. Early retirements, if you will.

You had to meet certain qualifications, and the editors had to decide to let you go. The requirements were 25 years with the paper and be at least 50 years old. If you met those requirements, and wanted to leave, you could take the Golden Parachute.

Since the job I had loved for more than 20 years was suddenly nothing more than punching a clock five nights a week, and education was calling to become my second career, I was a prime candidate.

There were a couple of ways you could accept the company's largesse. One was an increased pension, with major long-term benefits. The other was a lump sum based on two weeks salary for every year worked. Since I had a loan against my 401K pension plan – dating to my days of major financial insecurity – I had to take the later. That meant I was getting a check for about a year's salary ($48,000) before taxes. About $20k of that went to pay off the 401k loan, and I wound up with maybe $25,000 in severance.

I received that check on a Friday morning, from Human Resources, and was told I was done. They took my company key card (entrance to the building). I was technically still on the schedule for another Friday night of desk drudgery, but the H.R. lady made it clear I was out the door. I went back to sports, said a very stilted and cold goodbye to Whitley, picked up my few belongings, and was gone forever by noon. Yeah, I skipped out on one last desk shift, and had I cared about Whitley or the sports section he had wreaked havoc upon, I might have stayed to work.

But under the circumstances, I was gone. The *Daily Breeze* had been my work, my identity and my soul since December 1970, but on a spring day in 1998, I was out the door one last time.

On to education.

35

TEACHING WAS VERY, VERY GOOD TO ME (1998-2003)

For most of my life, I would never have imagined a job away from the newspaper world. But when it came time for a change, the commitment to teaching and education quickly changed my life.

For starters, I realized there were a lot of 20-somethings who were very smart, and many were going into teaching. But also, I realized that I could master this, even though I was starting late and playing catch-up.

The best thing that happened to me was the District Intern program run by the Los Angeles Unified School District. This was a program started during a previous shortage of teachers, that allowed you to earn your credential through district-run classes while earning a salary. The best part was the 6-week summer orientation which allowed me to start thinking like a teacher.

Because I had already accepted a teaching job in the spring (for Fall of 1998), I was able to attend the District Intern classes five days a week, roughly 8 a.m. to 3 p.m., without the worry of interviewing for a position. Like so many things in my life during the transition from newspaperman to teacher, this went surprisingly well.

Two of the reasons were the buyout (or early retirement) offered by *The Daily Breeze*, and receiving unemployment through the state for the four months between careers. Perhaps the most important: I rediscovered a lifelong love of learning.

The single biggest reason was the love and support of Nancy, who shouldered a lot of the burden of raising kids ages seven and two while working full time, so that I could make this change.

After leaving the *Daily Breeze* in April 1998, I finished up the classes at Cal State Dominguez Hills for my bachelor's degree in History. I received an "Outstanding Student" in History designation based on grades. Because I was nearly 30 years older than most graduates, and because the BA was more in the realm of unfinished business than a major accomplishment, I chose to skip the graduation.

In addition to preparing for and taking the entrance exams (MSAT for the District Intern program, CBEST to become a teacher in California), I also took a couple of basic Teacher Education classes at CSUDH that summer. Those helped prepare me for the District Intern Orientation which started in July.

In one of those classes, a fellow student also helped me understand the world I was entering: "It's been almost 10 years since graduation," he told the class. I didn't say it, but high school graduation was 33 years in my rear-view mirror at the time.

When I showed up at Daniel Webster Middle School in Palms (West L.A.) for the D.I. program, my life and my path got brighter. Waiting to meet me was another demographic anomaly to the program, Steve Braudo. He was in his 40s, and had left advertising to become a teacher. He also had young kids and a wife with a strong profession. He also had one advantage over me – he had actually taught for about three months, joining Caroldale as a long-term sub and teaching 4th grade that spring.

I was envious of his experience.

Steve and I were married by age, status as career changers and grade. He was teaching 4th grade in the classroom that connected to my 4th/5th Combo class. We figured out early in the first days of the D.I. program that by sticking together, we'd get through the long days and nights. We also started collecting friends for our unofficial but very necessary study group.

Nobody in the D.I. program ever said we needed to bond together, but we saw a need. The older teachers in the group started to gravitate to the two guys with gray hair and some mileage on their faces. We picked up a couple of older female teachers, Barbara Heughens and Jackie Friedman. We also added some talented young teachers, including Chrissie Schwartz, and our group grew stronger as we moved into the one-night-a-week classes.

The orientation was a marvelous way to bridge the gap from no experience to having a few tools in the toolbox to start off teaching elementary students. We learned how to manage a class, how to deliver instruction, and how to get along in a foreign world. And if you doubt the foreign aspects of a world of 8-year-olds, just go for a visit.

Years later, when I left the classroom to become a Teacher Advisor, then a Specialist, and finally Assistant Director of Recruiting and the District Intern Program for LAUSD, I would often return to the summer orientations to talk to the new teachers. I stressed that this was the best path to the career they had chosen, and talked about how Steve and I and our friends had gotten through the tasks.

During that summer as a teacher in training, I also learned that you would be assigned a mentor at your school. Steve and I wondered aloud if you were limited to one. Quickly we started collecting mentors. Anytime we met a teacher or administrator who knew something we wanted, we added them to the unofficial roster of mentors. Many became longtime friends and colleagues, including D.I. program administrator Janice Phelps, retired principal and UCLA sports fan George DaVall, and Carla Smotherman, the co-founder of the D.I. Program. Each would play a major role in my success as a teacher and later administrator.

But first came learning how to teach.

That was the hardest job I have ever undertaken. Nobody gives you "the secret" and tells you how things will work. They have a bad habit of giving you non-specific advice like, "everybody does it his or her own way," and "it depends on your personality."

I wanted The Answer, but nobody was giving.

Steve and I had to forge through the fall of 1998 and into the spring of 1999 before figuring that one out. We couldn't be like the 30-year veteran who taught 4th grade the same way she had for 30 years, pulling out folders for Week 9 or Week 10, and teaching it the same way as she had in the 1970s. Was she effective? Probably not, but it worked for her.

I also learned that the principal, at least ours, was only marginally interested in what was going on in the classrooms. Dennis Ebel, the Assistant Principal who had chaired my hiring committee, made it a point to come around occasionally. But I didn't see principal Patricia D'Andrea until late in the fall. And she was only escorting a guest from the district around and wanted to show off her gray-haired rookie teachers.

Later, I had a hands-on principal in Sharon Sweet, and that was more to my liking.

Mostly, though, beginning teachers are asked to be the lifeguards at a pool full of 9-year-olds, while learning to swim at the same time.

But our District Intern Classes – AKA Thursday Night Therapy – were essential. They taught us we weren't alone out there, and that every first-year teacher was going through the same difficulties. And that it would get better. Our study group thrived and each of us drew from the strength of the others. When it came time for group presentations, we knew who had what skills and we worked well together.

I also learned a lot about the organization of the D.I. Program, which led to some future benefits. By the end of the first year, I had convinced Dr. Janice Phelps to hire me as a $15-an-hour go-fer, helping her put on the next year's program. She went on to become my best mentor ever.

The next summer, I worked downtown in the Recruitment office for Carla Smotherman, once again as a low-paid staffer but with a chance to learn a lot.

Those summer jobs helped me get a broader perspective on teaching, education in general, and the giant world of LAUSD. I continued to take summer jobs throughout my five years in the classroom.

My first year required juggling a mixed class of 4th and 5th graders, while trying to learn how to teach. That taught me a few invaluable lessons. In split classes, the lower grade students are generally top of their grade, while the upper graders are more towards the bottom of their group, thus narrowing the gap. I also learned that as an administrator, I would never assign a combo class to a beginning teacher.

My second year, I had all 4th graders, confirming my belief that 9-year-old kids don't have much of a sense of humor. I was becoming a passable elementary teacher, while learning I really didn't want to be an elementary teacher.

At the end of our second year, we graduated from the District Intern program, receiving California Clear Credentials. In my case that was for multiple subjects, allowing me to teach through grade 8, with some complications.

At the graduation ceremony at Hollywood High School, I received the Golden Apple Award as top student in my cohort. I had worked hard, and this was the reward. Later, I hired a new recruiter who would become a close friend, Luz Ortega, and found out she was the Golden Apple winner of the high school cohort that same day, making the honor even more special.

I learned that the nearby Carson High was looking for an English teacher, and unaware of the credentialing rules, thought that might me my next stop. I interviewed with the principal, and might have been headed in that direction, but some other options came up. I also was scheduled for an interview at the Wiseburn School District in Hawthorne, which was looking for a middle school teacher.

But on the day of that interview, assistant principal Dennis Ebel offered me a chance to move to Caroldale's middle school to teach English/History core classes. That was the offer I needed. I canceled the trip to Hawthorne, gave up on trying to solve the high school credential problem, and moved to the ranks where I was destined to succeed.

I had left my buddy Steve Braudo, although we remained friends, and found a different world in the middle school. I realized what every educator has known for years – middle school kids (roughly 11 to 13 or 14) have very short attention spans. But that worked for me, since my attention span was that of a gnat, too.

In middle school, I started out with two double-block classes of 6th graders, meaning I had about an hour and 40 minutes to teach them English and Social Studies each day. It was my choice how to split the time and the lessons. I also had two electives, which quickly became journalism and P.E.

By my third year in teaching, I was in hog heaven. I loved what I was doing, and was getting pretty good at it. I also had summer work each year, moving to the District Intern program a third time, then joining an offshoot of Teach for America (called Teach in L.A.) and was executive director of their summer training program. It was a chance to put to work everything I'd learned from the D.I. program.

I had to hire about 10 teachers to head up my summer classrooms for beginning teachers. One of those was my niece, Toriann Raber, who had taught music for two years at Beverly Hills High School.

Once again, I was moving fast, helping design the curriculum for new teachers, a lesson plan for their instruction, and monitoring their progression through the program. This was just four years after I had left journalism for teaching. I learned a lot about administration that summer, and my appetite was whetted for another big leap.

When I returned to Caroldale for my fifth year, and third in the middle school, I felt very good about my new life. Not only was I getting pretty good at teaching, I was moving up the pay scale. Teaching is the only job where you can give yourself pay raise by taking classes.

After two years of D.I. classes added up to two or three raises, I started taking correspondence courses (precursor to online classes) and piled on the units. I also started a Masters in Education program at CSUDH after my second year of teaching. All of which helped me move toward the top of the stack in units (98 for LAUSD) while moving over in steps (years). I went from earning $32,000 as a beginning teacher to nearly doubling that salary in my fifth year. And I was earning about $15,000 each summer on part-time jobs with the district.

By the way, I was often asked how much I enjoyed those summers off as a teacher. I had no good answer, since I never took a summer off. I found district-related summer work which helped me advance in my new career.

Although content with my world, I was always looking for options. And when Carla Smotherman was allowed to add a Teacher Advisor to her staff at District Intern recruiting, I was sure that job was for me. It was a pay raise, and switch to regular working hours, and a foot in the door to becoming an administrator.

Once again, things were lining up just right for me. Right time, right place. Lucky? Sure. But I was ready for the next move.

MOVING DOWNTOWN
WITH LAUSD (2003)

Five years in the classroom was the minimum for any administrative job at Los Angeles Unified School District. Like a lot of things in my new career, I was getting in just under the wire.

In my five years at Caroldale: I taught a 4th/5th combo, 4th grade, 6th Grade English/Social Studies twice, and 6th grade Math/Science once. There were also electives at the Middle School, where I had found a home. We taught six periods out of a seven-period day. So, my best year was two of the double-period core classes, plus one elective each for journalism and P.E.

And while I would have been happy making a career at Caroldale, the wanderlust was constantly catching my attention. Each of the four summers between school years, I worked for some form of the district, either the Intern Program, or Human Resources Recruitment, or the new teacher project called Teach in L.A. These jobs opened doors and showed me there was so much more to education than just teaching. I also learned that the path to financial success and administrative challenge was not necessarily at the school site. I was beginning to doubt whether being a principal was going to be my path.

So, when a position was created for a Teacher Advisor in the District Intern Program in Recruitment, I figured it was made for me. Teacher

Advisors are still on the teacher pay scale instead of the administrative scale, but work more hours. It winds up being about a 20 percent jump in gross pay, but you are working a year-round schedule.

I arrived on a Monday, started meeting co-workers, and learning about the job, while putting my desk in order.

Then I called in sick on Tuesday. For six weeks.

Talk about an auspicious debut.

In addition to starting a new job that July, we were having our roof replaced. After dinner on Monday, I wanted to go up and take a look at what was happening. Normally I would have asked Randy, then 11, to accompany me on this manly chore. But he was assigned to do dishes, and, as always, I was impatient.

I picked up the long ladder that the workers had left, placed it against the house, and climbed up. I got to the edge of the roof when the ladder slipped out from under me, and I was left to fall in a prone position about 10 feet to the garden, bricks, and cement below me. Among other things, I was breathless. I also was pretty sure I'd done some serious damage. But I couldn't speak.

Nancy and the kids quickly arrived, and called the paramedics from the fire department, which was only a few blocks away. While laying on the ground in major pain, I knew things were bad. One of the firemen offered me morphine to cut the pain and I turned it down. I was still very aware of my life as a recovering addict, and didn't want to start a pain addiction. Wrong call. Fortunately, they asked a second time, and I accepted.

A trip to Little Company of Mary Hospital followed – Nancy overruled them when they wanted to send me to Harbor General, the County Hospital, because of a possible head injury. There was a long night in the emergency room, an E.R. nurse named Tigger who had lots of tattoos, and several shots of morphine as well as Xrays. Then came a midnight surgery to repair the fractured elbow. Surprisingly, my right hip wasn't broken.

I woke up the next day in a hospital bed and called my new boss, Carla Smotherman, to report my mishap. I was on sick leave at home for six weeks, not only because of the broken elbow, but a later infection I picked up from being in the hospital.

That mishap created a family legend when someone would say I fell off the ladder, and I would correct them. The ladder left me. I didn't fall.

Turns out ladders like that have one end that goes on the ground, and remains stationary, and one end that points to the sky. I put the wrong end down.

There was a miserable stretch of staying home, and getting some super antibiotic dripped into my arm. It arrived via a home-health nurse, who expected me to handle the self-injections. Fortunately, Nancy was skilled in this area, and was able to handle the daily infusions.

When I returned to my new job, there was a second wave of introductions, and learning what I was doing. There was also a major chore for one of the secretaries: Figuring out how I was going to be paid for the six weeks. Teacher pay is complicated and includes regular pay, sick pay and half-pay, which I knew nothing about. Only in education does everyone receive up to 100 days of half-pay when their sick days have run out.

After all that, I started learning from the legendary Carla Smotherman, co-founder of the state's first and most successful teacher intern program. She was one of my first mentors, a strong woman who knew how to work the system. I also got to meet a number of powerful and impressive people in a stint that would last nearly six years.

While my initial job was learning about the program, how to recruit for it, and how to work the LAUSD system, I was also in a great position to learn from some excellent administrators.

I learned how to be a leader from Carolina Pavia, a strong woman who came to LAUSD after working her way to the top as superintendent of a smaller district. She was ultimately at the top of my chain of command, but she seemed to take a special interest in my career. She said it was because we were both outsiders and not of the traditional LAUSD clan, but we were also about the same age (late 50s, early 60s). She was my best downtown mentor, and it was her advice I sought six years later when I was trying to decide on an offer to leave LAUSD for the much smaller Centinela Valley Union High School District.

The 15th Floor at LAUSD was a hotbed of brilliant folks and I had daily opportunities to learn. Not only from the bosses, which I would later join, but also the bright young classified workers who seemed to know how to do everything., Several of them would later become lasting friends. Jennifer Dominguez and Brandi Alvarez were part of the group of HR-1s, who handled all manner of chores for the recruiters, including mining the internet for candidates, and planning recruitment events. Later, Jennifer became my H.R. Manager at CV and Brandi joined us as an analyst,

I found stimulation and challenge constantly during my time at LAUSD. I learned how to recruit teachers from a cast of great recruiters. I learned to read applications, and I learned how to plan events. I picked the brains of everyone on the floor, shamelessly mining the wealth of knowledge.

I loved the job and quickly became the first to arrive in the morning (beating traffic, among other things), and one of the last to leave, mostly because there was a great chance to meet with other managers at the end of the day.

My long-held philosophy that arriving early had no down-side worked well at the Beaudry Building.

I developed a lifestyle that was very comfortable in six years at the headquarters of LAUSD. Our offices were on the 15th floor of a 30-story building. At least once every day – usually lunch – I would take the stairs down rather than riding the elevator. And every so often, I would climb the 15 stories just to show I could.

For lunch, most days, I would take off and walk 45 minutes to an hour around downtown Los Angeles, giving me an insight into the city that I had never fully appreciated. I found a small clothing shop in a mall and bought a number of suits and sport coats there.

I learned about technology from Arnie Weiner, another mentor for many years. I followed his path through several jobs, including Disaster Coordinator for the entire H.R. floor.

Carla Smotherman was the co-founder of the District Intern Program, along with Mary Lewis, and was a legend in recruitment and educational ranks. Hers was a name that meant something when you dropped it. But she was not in good health in her late 60s, and started missing a lot of work. That put me in the position of filling in for her, and my learning curve was accelerating. A position for a Specialist was created and I applied and was chosen. That moved me to the administrative ranks and was another pay raise. I was earning more than $100k a year seven years after I started teaching at $32k.

I also needed help with my 401K and other retirement funds, and Carla's son, Bob Smotherman, was an investment counselor. He and I would begin a relationship that continues to this day as he steered me through several critical financial decisions.

As a specialist, I was on a par with all but the top managers, and was getting more and more responsibility for the D.I. Program, but also our parallel mission of recruitment.

When Carla passed away, I was chosen as one of the pallbearers, which was a considerable honor since she had mentored, taught and advised hundreds of new teachers over the years, but I was the one she brought into the office in her later years.

Although office politics prevented Carla from becoming an Assistant Director, once she passed away, her position was upgraded. Arnie Weiner, a long-time all-around star in the office and another mentor, was chosen for the position. Although he knew everything about the computer systems, and most aspects of H.R., he was a little thin on District Intern knowledge, which meant we became close.

After a year or so with Arnie as the Assistant Director/District Intern Program, he was promoted to another spot. And I was encouraged to apply for the position.

Perhaps because of her understanding of office politics, Carolina Pavia put herself in charge of the interview panel, along with Mary Lewis, who I had worked for and with since becoming a District Intern. Absent from the panel was Debi Ignagni, director of recruitment, who apparently was not fond of me. After the interviews, Carolina called me on the phone and told me I was the choice, but that I could not tell a soul that afternoon. In fact, she said, take the rest of the day off and we'll announce things in the morning.

My climb from the classroom to a window office on the 15th Floor at LAUSD was complete. From $32k to $115K in less than 10 years. I was pretty ecstatic on the drive home.

The next two years, as one of three assistant directors in Recruitment, were among the best in my work career. The other assistants were Don Hafeman, who taught me everything about handling difficult situations, but fell short in office politics, and Barbara Burnett, who was in charge of Special Education recruitment. We worked under Ignagni, but also under

Carolina Pavia. Additionally, since I was in charge of recruitment for the D.I. Program, I was technically assistant director to Mary Lewis.

Overall leadership in H.R. went to a former Navy Captain named Roger Buschmann. For reasons that may have included our shared military background, he was fond of me as well. Later, when I decided to leave for CVUHSD, Roger gave me a leave of absence to cover the 2½ year length of my CV contract. It was the longest leave ever granted to an administrator in H.R. at LAUSD. I guess you could say I left on good terms.

Roger later departed for Northern California and became Superintendent of the San Francisco Unified School District.

After my departure, LAUSD went through a lot of changes, and there was no way of telling whether my euphoric time at Beaudry would have lasted. Many changes happened that would not have been good for me.

But from the day I arrived – before calling in sick for six weeks – 'til the day I departed 5½ years later, it was the greatest ride I ever had and the best working situation. I was around a lot of great people, constantly challenged, constantly learning, and moving up the ladder.

NEW DISTRICT, NEW
CHALLENGES (2008-2015)

One of the things I learned in spades at LAUSD was Customer Service. I learned it from Carolina Pavia, from Carla Smotherman, from Don Hafeman, from Luz Ortega and from so many other talented Human Resources professionals.

It was a normal part of my day when I was asked to help a librarian at Lawndale High who wanted to become a teacher. A long-time friend, Mike Pardridge, was interested in becoming an administrator and I was helping him figure out the ropes. Along the way, he mentioned he was teaching English at Lawndale High School in the Centinela Valley Union High School District, in the South Bay.

During one of our calls, Pardridge asked if I could help librarian Gloria Ramos through the paces. She was in her mid-30s, was just finishing up her BA at Cal State Northridge, and wanted to make the big jump from classified school employee to teacher. Pardridge knew how I had made a career switch and become credentialed through the District Intern program.

This was pretty much what I did in those days, helping folks to find the right path if they wanted to become an educator. It wasn't above and beyond, but part of my regular routine as a recruiter. I talked to Ms. Ramos a half dozen times over perhaps a year. I coached her on the CBEST and CSET tests, and sold her on the District Intern program. All on the phone.

When she finally achieved the trifecta (Bachelor's degree, CBEST and CSET passage), I congratulated her and got her on the interview schedule for one of our recruiters, George Gonzalez. Again, nothing out of the ordinary. I never actually met her in person until after her interview. Once approved by Gonzalez for the D.I. program, Gloria Ramos and I met briefly. Later I met her a couple of times during her Orientation program, and when she was finding a teaching job.

She was one of dozens, maybe even hundreds, who I helped become a teacher over my years as a Teacher Advisor, Recruitment Specialist, and Assistant Director. But she was the only one who ever offered me a job.

In the Fall of 2007, Ramos and a couple of other Lawndale residents ran for the school board of the tiny Centinela Valley Union High School District and won seats. She led the majority on a split board, 3-2 on everything, that wanted to oust Superintendent Cheryl White. Their feeling was that the small district (three high schools, a continuation school, and an adult education program) could be much better than it was.

Ramos was in her second year as a teacher at Audubon Middle School in LAUSD, when she called me one night and wondered if I might be interested in coming to work for CVUHSD as an assistant superintendent of human resources. I was floored, but intrigued. I had a very good job as assistant director of recruitment, but had probably reached my very comfortable ceiling. I was making about $115k and loved my work.

But I was also driving 45 minutes to an hour each way into downtown Los Angeles. And CVUHSD was about 15 minutes from my home, on surface streets.

Since Ramos and Sandra Suarez were elected in November, and were being installed on the board in December, she was moving fast. She had a new superintendent in mind in Jose Fernandez, who had been fired as Assistant Superintendent of Business months earlier by White. On the night in December when the new three-woman majority took over, they fired the longtime superintendent on a 3-2 vote. Rocio Pisano was a carryover board member who joined them in the majority. Rudy Suarez and Frank Talavera were in the minority on this and nearly every other vote for the next two years.

The money was part of the attraction (a gain of more than $20,000 a year), although I was making more than I'd ever imagined and did not think that was a reason to move. The chance to be completely in charge of human resources and to help a new team turn things around, were the major attractions.

On the night I was hired, *The Daily Breeze*, my newspaper home for 25 years, played the story of my hiring across the top of the inside front (page A-3) and the headline roared with what my old colleagues thought: CV hires Bob Cox for $142K Job.

Yeah, they were stunned. So was I.

I met Jose Fernandez at a private breakfast in West L.A. as he and I were vetted by Ramos and her friends on the leadership team of the CV teacher union. That was the group that wanted to oust Superintendent White and who rallied behind their librarian friend Gloria Ramos in the election.

School Board positions are not usually a way to get rich. They pay about $250 a month (for attending meetings) plus some expenses. But they wield a lot of power, especially in small communities like Lawndale, Hawthorne, and the unincorporated County territory of Lennox, where CVUHSD managed three high schools.

It was a whirlwind start, and I was taking over a department run by a former best-pal and crony of White, Marlene Pitchford. I was not popular when I arrived, and I had a lot to learn.

At big districts like LAUSD, folks in H.R. specialize. I was a recruitment expert, for example. But I knew little about benefits, credentials, or negotiations. At small districts, like CVUHSD, you need to be a master of everything. My first year was a crash course in all those things. Not to mention how to conduct layoffs, how to work with and manage a board, and how to reshape and improve an educational product that needed help.

I was thrust into the lead role in collective bargaining with the teachers union and the classified employees union. This was like jumping into the deep end on your first day of swimming lessons. Collective bargaining follows form and everyone knows their role in this scripted exercise. I thought it was like buying a used car: What's your best offer? It was a struggle to learn, but with the help of lawyer Candace Bandoian, I managed to tread water until I learned to swim.

I also got a crash course in the contract status of administrative employees in school districts, as taught by the master, Jose Fernandez. His mastery of contracts would eventually get him fired and set up a trial date for summer 2020 as he was charged with misappropriation of public funds and a few other felonies.

Early on, I realized I would be learning from Fernandez. I just didn't know how much.

After about half a year as an interim superintendent, making the same salary as I was, Fernandez convinced the board to hire him as the superintendent, with a major pay raise. His first contract included a lot of perks. After its approval by the board, he dropped a copy off in my office. I jokingly said, "Give me a couple of hours to find where all the money is hidden." Fernandez was not joking when he said, "You'll never find all the money."

Years later, when he was investigated, then fired, then arrested, I started to realize the truth in what he said.

Jose Fernandez and I would be together on the management team at CVUHSD for more than 6 years. Later, when his troubles began, one of the District Attorney's investigators asked me about my relationship with Fernandez., I said we didn't have one: He was the superintendent and I was his assistant.

In six plus years, we never went out to lunch. We did not get together socially, nor did we become friends.

We did have a wild ride.

His background was mostly in adult education, with a short stint as assistant superintendent of business. He was connected to a number of Hispanics who worked in local politics, which included a lot of big fish in small ponds, like CV.

While my expertise was in hiring teachers, I started to learn about hiring administrators, dealing with unions, conducting layoffs, attending to discipline of both certificated and classified staff, and everything else that constitutes H.R.

Fortunately, we had a great relationship with our law firm, and I was able to lean on Bandoian and Sue Ann Salmon Evans when I stumbled into the many areas where I lacked experience.

Since Fernandez' interest was in money, bond issues, building construction and the like, I pretty much had a free hand in matters of H.R. Much like I felt when I was at various junctures along the way, once again I had the best job I could have ever imagined.

And every so often, Fernandez would propose contract renewals for us (and the two other assistant supes), so that I was never coming up on the end of a contract. My contract at CV expired only once, when I ran afoul of the board president during my year as Interim Supe, and that led to my retirement after 7½ years.

I was able to build a powerful and well-oiled machine in H.R., making it a department that easily ran itself. That's what I told Principal Mike Ono when I hand-picked him for my job when it was clear I would be retiring in 2015.

F * C K CANCER (2012-2013)

That's the message on the back of a sweatshirt Nancy and the kids made for me after my Bataan Death March with the disease. On the front it says "Survivor x 2" indicating both the throat cancer that nearly tackled me and the major skin cancer that caused an infection and led to an unsightly skin graft on my left leg.

Skin cancer has been a lifelong battle, mostly starting with the way my generation approached the sun and tanning. We loved the sun and craved the golden-brown tans that came with prolonged and repeated exposure. If you weren't tan, you weren't healthy, at least that was our approach in the 1960s and '70s and into the '80s.

When I started at *The Daily Breeze* in December 1970, we moved to a 2-bedroom apartment on Paseo de la Playa in Redondo Beach. We were a half-block from the ocean and a set of volleyball courts. Since I was working mostly nights in the 1970s, either working the desk, or covering boxing, baseball or an assortment of other sports, I had a lot of time on my hands.

Volleyball became a passion and I was on the beach 100 plus days a year. While I became a passably good volleyball player, despite a lack of height, I also acquired and maintained a killer tan. Sunscreen was just coming into the world in those days, but we lived by a simple mantra regarding our tans: Get a good burn early, then let it sink in with repeated exposure.

Skin cancer may have been a reality, but it was not talked about in our world.

Not surprisingly, later in life, I started seeing the evidence of decades of skin abuse. I'd see a skin doctor periodically, and they'd freeze off a few of the pre-cancerous cells. But one visit to a dermatologist in about 2010 dealt with a growth on my left calf.

The plan was to have the skin doc cut off a growth about the size of a nickel, and his partner plastic surgeon would stitch it up. Somewhere in the process, they botched the job. I wound up with a massively swollen leg and was back in their office several times in the next two days for repair jobs. They were even sneaking me in via the employee entrance, since they didn't want their beautiful clients to see the mess they'd made.

I wound up in Torrance Memorial Hospital's emergency room on the weekend with an infection that required several hours on an IV with a major antibiotic, and was referred by the hospital to a wound care specialist. That led to prolonged treatment and eventually two surgeries to graft skin from my thigh to the wound on my calf that had grown from the size of a nickel to about the size of a dollar bill folded in half.

The doctors who botched the surgery quietly referred me to an ombudsman in their practice, and I never paid a nickel (pun intended) for the ensuing hospital visits and surgeries. They knew my damages weren't enough for any lawyer to take the case, but they also knew they were the reason for the problems.

But that was just an introduction to cancer.

Cancer with a capital C arrived in the fall of 2012. I had been rubbing an odd bump on my left jaw line for weeks, maybe months, wondering about it. But not doing anything.

When I finally asked my general practice doctor about it, he referred me to an ear, nose and throat specialist. I wound up seeing Dr. Yamadala and I loved the fact he started seeing patients at 6:30 in the morning. I could see him and still get to work on time.

I loved the early appointments. But 6:45 in the morning is not a great time to learn you have Stage 4 throat cancer. Not a lot of folks you can call at that time.

After a series of tests, I was referred to a doctor at USC Norris Cancer Center who specialized in throat cancers. He started with a procedure (under anesthesia) to scope out the cancer. He then went back to his colleague, Dr. Barbara Gitlin, and they went to the cancer screening board at USC. It was decided I could avoid surgery – although that was what the surgeon wanted – by undergoing radiation and chemotherapy.

Thus, began the lost winter for me. Starting before Thanksgiving, and ending shortly after January, I was driving to USC's sprawling medical campus on the east side of downtown L.A. five times a week for 30 minutes of radiation. Thirty minutes seems like such a modest time frame. Counting the drive from the South Bay during traffic, parking, getting prepared for the radiation, and getting home, it was more like three hours. And I was always exhausted.

There were also six separate trips to another USC hospital downtown for the chemo sessions, which lasted six hours each and took place in a hospital room.

Cancer survivors have a lot of jokes about chemo – sick humor, to be sure – but radiation was the deadliest opponent for me. The two combined to kill the Stage 4 cancers in my saliva glands and on my throat, but it was not an easy fight.

Chemo is basically a cocktail of poisonous drugs that kill all the evil cancer cells – and a lot of other cells – in your body. Radiation is also a killer in a different way. It burns out the bad cells and a lot of others. I still have burn marks on the skin of my neck, for example.

Chemo is known for killing brain cells and wiping out great gobs of memory. Cancer survivors excuse their lack of memory by referring to Chemo Brain. I used to say that I spent the first 40 years of my life killing brain cells the old-fashioned way, with Scotch Whisky. Then I made six visits to the Chemo Bar to finish the job. Any memory I had left was purely accidental.

But the radiation knocked me on my butt every day, five days a week. And it only took 30 minutes.

At my first appointment, a technician fitted me for a ceramic mask, which allowed them to focus the deadly radiation rays on the part of my face and neck that needed the most killing. I was intimidated, and frightened from the fitting of the mask on. I never looked at the mask from beginning to the end of the treatment. I never said much, and was terrified of the process every day.

My fears were mostly internalized, since I didn't want to scare the kids. Randy was in his third year at Northern Arizona University, while Allie was a junior at West Torrance High. They had their own worlds to deal with. Nancy's matter-of-fact approach to all things scientific and medical allowed us to have an open conversation, but I wasn't very good about sharing my fears and my worries.

I was also bull-headed enough – no surprise here, right? – to insist on continuing to work, and to drive myself to the USC Medical Campus on the east side of downtown, and to drive back to work. While the radiation was killing cancer cells on my throat, it was also turning my throat into a restricted passage. I could not get food down, and was losing weight by the boatload.

Within a week or two, noticing my weakness and my inability to eat, the doctors decided to fit me with a feeding tube. They inserted an external tube into my stomach surgically, and sent me a case or two of liquid that I was supposed to pour in four times a day. Sort of like 12-ounce cans of poorly tasting chocolate milk. I rarely got all 4 cans down on any given day, and the weight loss continued.

The radiation had constricted my throat to the point I could barely get a few sips of water down. Because I could not even swallow the canned protein drinks, I needed the feeding tube. I was becoming a shadow of my formerly confident self, both physically and emotionally.

I was not able to wear most of my suits – size 42, waist 36. I bought one sports coat and two pair of off-the-rack slacks in my new sizes (coat 39 and waist 32 pants) to get me through. Although I did know what was at the other end of the tunnel. I was very much living day-to-day and not projecting ahead.

I certainly could not face the possibility that Cancer would take me out, and certainly I could not talk to anyone about it. About the extent of my acknowledgement of the possibility was a folder I put together for Nancy, called "Only if … " That covered things like life insurance, and other money matters if Nancy was suddenly required to deal with them.

I was surely ineffective at work – fortunately, I had a great crew in Human Resources at CVUHSD – and I was pretty much a zombie through the holidays. I could barely swallow a few sips of water, and my meals consisted of pouring the liquid protein into the tube.

My staff carried the load through the holidays, and while I was at work and in my office nearly every day, it's hard to imagine what I was getting done. Fortunately, the holidays are usually slow periods in school districts.

I don't want to ask Nancy or the kids what it was like being around me then, but I know I was not a treat. I was crabby, depressed, weakened and moody. Mostly I spent my time at home in the recliner in the den. I was pretty much a hermit at Christmas 2012.

When the treatments had run their course in late January, I was going in for testing regularly. One particularly unpleasant test involved sticking a tube up my nose and down my throat so the doctor could look at the burned-out cancer. These tests continued annually until spring 2020 when the corona virus led to a virtual visit for my check-up.

I was still eating the liquid diet, and my weight had dropped from about 195 to about 140. I didn't tell anyone, but at one point, my weight bottomed out at 138 pounds. Emaciated was a good way to put it.

That March, our group of ski writers (NASJA) was holding its annual meeting at Lake Tahoe, which I had planned and put together as I had the previous 20 NASJA annual meetings. But I was certainly not capable of skiing. I flew to Reno and took a shuttle bus to our hotel at South Shore. Before the trip, I shipped a box of my liquid meals to the hotel. I went for just three nights, rather than five, and was very aware of my weakened status.

I was determined to ski, at least a little. When we picked up our rental skis, and were walking to the gondola, it was obvious I did not have the strength to carry my skis. Phil Johnson, a longtime friend and fellow past president of the organization, quietly carried my equipment. I was able to make one intermediate run with Phil, his wife Brigitte, Frida Waara, and a couple of other pals.

I was exhausted, but thrilled. I had skied. Six months after the diagnosis of throat cancer, I was able to at least ski one run. I went back to my room, drank my liquid meal and took a nap. I took a lot of naps in those days.

The next day was a bus ride to Sierra Summit, and another one-run day. But I was accomplishing something. I was seeing the light at the end of the tunnel. During the two months of treatment, I didn't admit it to anyone, but I was not certain that light existed. I might never ski again, or enjoy any of life's other pleasures.

By skiing a couple of runs at the NASJA meeting, I was acknowledging the sun that signals the end of winter and means it is March, always my favorite month.

I had started to learn how to eat again from an eating therapist who realized that having not eaten anything orally in three months, I was terrified at the prospect. We started out with a tiny bite of apple sauce. What a thrill! A bit of apple sauce, and not much else. But I was still in the baby stages of learning to eat again. So, at the NASJA banquet, I pushed a few items around my plate, and enjoyed being there in the company of Joani Lynch, the marketing director at Mammoth and another longtime friend.

As weakened as I was, I was also swimming in both my ski clothes and my regular clothes because of the 50-plus pounds I had shed. To all of the friends who helped me attend that NASJA meeting, know that it was one of the most important parts of my return to the real world.

The next day, I took the shuttle back to Reno for the airplane ride home.

The biggest battle for the next month was ending the stomach tube feedings and learning to eat once again. That was a long and tedious battle. My throat had constricted to a fraction of its normal size and mine truly were baby bites.

But from apple sauce came other easily swallowed foods, and I was able to have them remove the tube. I started looking for food items not based on taste, but on ease of digestion. That remains true to this day as I eat a lot of pasta.

My weight stabilized at about 150 pounds, and I eventually replaced my entire wardrobe (six suits, six sport coats and slacks, plus many dress shirts). The only thing I didn't have to replace were the ties.

A lot of colleagues and good friends helped me through the cancer battle. Some helped by pretending to not notice what a wreck I had become. Some helped by ignoring what an unpleasant sort I was to be around. Nancy was her usual positive self, and pulled both her load and mine in keeping the family on track. The kids were both taking care of business in high school and in college.

When asked their memories about that period, all three confirm they pretty much focused on the positive things and tried to ignore the negative. That was certainly my approach as well.

Cancer remains on my dance card, with regular visits to the skin doctor for past and current sins.

I also have a new opponent in a type of blood cancer that is pretty much a precursor to leukemia. It's controlled by an expensive drug called Jakafi, and mercifully paid for by Medicare and other insurance. Good thing, too, since it retails for $11,000 per month. But I have another doc who takes early appointments – 7 o'clock with Dr. Mak – and the news has not been any worse than the original diagnosis.

During the corona virus pandemic of 2020, though, I was reminded constantly that I was a high-risk patient with a compromised immune system. Nothing new there, but I treated this challenge with respect and avoided risky behavior.

MY YEAR AS INTERIM
SUPERINTENDENT (2014-2015)

My relationship with Jose Fernandez was as professional as it was distant. We had virtually nothing in common, save for our jobs at Centinela Valley Union High School District.

Fernandez, had spent most of his career in Adult Education – one of the backwaters of secondary education – and was previously fired by CV Superintendent Cheryl White from his position as Assistant Superintendent for Business Services. He was on the outside, running an import/export business when he helped Gloria Ramos and Sandra Suarez get elected to the Board.

Although I had never heard of him, Jose had been on the edges for a while. He was appointed to a vacant spot on the Inglewood City Council years earlier. He was elected once, then turned out by the voters. Inglewood was significant since it was the only City Council (besides Los Angeles) that paid its elected leaders a living wage. All of the others received modest stipends for attending meetings, perhaps $200 or $300 a month.

Fernandez learned many political lessons in Inglewood, which was believed to be among the most corrupt of the low-rent cities. After the voters declined to keep Fernandez, he was appointed, and later elected to a seat on the Water Board. Another Who Cares job, right? Except it paid $150,000 a year, plus expenses.

Inglewood's public image has improved recently with the building of the football stadium for the Rams and Chargers and the upgrading of the surrounding area.

Fernandez was also an aide to somebody in the state Assembly. In short, he was within sniffing distance of power for a long time, but always out of the public eye.

His connection to education included a couple of years as a high school teacher at Long Beach Wilson High. His highest rank was Director of Activities. When he was employed at CV, it was always in Adult Ed, another dumping ground where corruption flourished in most districts.

When we were united at CV at the behest of Gloria Ramos, Fernandez arrived as Interim Superintendent, but also had the permanent rank (and salary) of Assistant Superintendent for Adult Ed. He made it a great point to remind me that he was making the same money ($142k) as I was. But he was putting to work all the lessons he'd learned in his corruption under-grad work at Sacramento, Inglewood and on the Water Board.

He taught me a lot of things, including mathematics. Three was the most important number, as in three votes on a 5-member School Board. Rudy Suarez and Frank Talavera, the minority, could object all they wanted to any proposal we were pushing, but as long as Gloria, Sandra and Rocio were smiling, Jose would get what he wanted.

Things got easier in the next election, when Jose and his advisors found a couple of more amenable board candidates, and suddenly we had a powerful 5-0 Board. That's when a lot of things were passed such as Fernandez's various contract extensions and modifications. We also entered into a lot of agreements in those days. The voters passed $200 million in bond issues to rebuild our aging schools.

Power came in a lot of ways. Fernandez understood that one of the ways he could wield power was by passing bonds, and signing contracts with giant construction companies to rebuild our facilities. He loved the contract game – the deals that ultimately helped make CV a better district. But which also indebted the home owners of Hawthorne, Lawndale and the L.A. County territory we served, for hundreds of millions.

Fernandez loved construction. That's why he invited the president of the construction company to sit on the cabinet. Rare was the Tuesday cabinet meeting when time was not spent on construction talk. And I was tuning out. Either worrying about teacher hiring, layoffs, sports teams, or something similar.

The various Assistant Supes for Ed Services were usually with me on the tune-out for construction talk. Only Ron Hacker, the business guy, seemed as interested in the building game as Jose.

All of which led to one of the great ironies of my final year at CV. We were completing one building on each campus during the year when I was Interim Superintendent. When a new building is opened in the public sector, there is a brass plaque that commemorates the completion. It mentions the date, the school Board President and members, and the Superintendent. At first, I did not want my name on these, but when the construction guy suggested it, I went along. So, for the next 50 years or more there will be a plaque on each campus honoring the Superintendent when the building was completed – the guy who had the least interest in the building project of any of the district administrators. Me.

While Jose was interested in consolidating his power, and increasing his take-home pay, I was taking care of the business of rebuilding the district. Much of that was focused on hiring better teachers. In my 7½ years at CV, we turned over half of the teachers. Did we improve things? Immeasurably.

We also ran successful searches for new administrators at all campuses, and grew a number of young assistant principals into bright educational leaders.

I also learned about the power of collective bargaining and how to negotiate on the district's side. We pushed through a couple of layoffs – including the mandatory hearings to make sure we laid off teachers by the book. We handled grievances, arbitration and a lot of other processes.

At the beginning, I was dog-paddling in the deep end of the pool, trying to learn the skills that were foreign to me when I came to CV. While I learned a lot from Fernandez, my best tutors were usually our district lawyers. Candace Bandoian and Sue Ellen Salmon Evans were my frequent mentors. They knew school law like the experts they were. And Jose was never shy about running up legal bills. So, I was constantly on the phone to them, trying to increase my knowledge.

In the final year at CV, when their firm was considered a potential defendant in the multiple charges against Fernandez, we were forced to switch firms. I was able to make that work, since the lawyers at the new firm were professional. But their expertise was in municipal settings and they were learning school law on the fly. I missed Candace and Sue Ellen.

When the boat started leaking in 2014, the attacks came from the most surprising source. *The Daily Breeze* education reporter was a nice enough fellow with limited education credentials in Rob Kuznia. But the *Breeze* had a longtime city editor named Frank Suraci, who I had known for years. And under Suraci's guidance, and with help from some other staffers, they were able to start pulling on the strings.

It started with someone at L.A. County Office of Education suggesting that Fernandez's gross salary was significantly larger than the $235,000 published. Like double or triple. The Breeze published a combined salary and benefits package of $650,000 – and later upped it to more than $700,000 – and they were right. By asking the right questions, they suddenly had a gigantic local story. After a few weeks of *Breeze* scoops, even the *L.A. Times* felt the need to jump in, although they were always following the *Breeze.*

At first, I was trying to serve as district spokesman, but Fernandez wanted more of a forceful voice, and hired a political damage control outfit to serve as his spokesman and speech writer. But I was sitting in on the meetings. Then the Board realized that this was a sinking ship, and sought outside counsel.

After several contentious months, they realized that a superintendent making more than every school superintendent in America except for New York City, was not going to play well. Particularly since our three schools were in one of the lowest income areas of Southern California. How could the Superintendent of a district no one had ever heard of be making twice what the leader of L.A. Unified was making?

Suddenly our board meetings were can't-miss events, and they were filling up the Performing Arts Center at Lawndale High. We needed extra security and the meetings went on for hours.

Eventually, the Board fired Fernandez, and I was chosen Interim Superintendent. I could have taken on the trappings of the office, but continued to work out of my office in H.R. We also commissioned a head-hunting firm to seek a permanent new Supe.

I was not interested, which made me the ideal interim supe. I was not auditioning for the job, but rather, cleaning up the mess before the new guy would ride in on a white horse.

As Interim, I was like the guy who follows the horses in the parade and cleans up the poop. We got rid of a couple of Jose's special hires, guys who reported only to him. We also tightened the reins on a lot of questionable expenditures involving the Board.

Empowered by a sense of getting things right, I started seeking legal opinions on the things I knew would continue to haunt the board. One of Fernandez' first moves was to give the contract employees (superintendent and assistant supes) a monthly mileage allowance of $600. That was up from the previous cap of $200. His goal was to give it to the board members as well, but to do this, the lawyers told him it had to be available to the highest non-contract administrators, or directors. One day early on, the principals, assistant principals, and directors, all received the news that they would be receiving a $600 monthly allowance.

Now put this in perspective. Our district was about a mile and a half from end to end. If you drove a lap between the schools, it might be 2½ miles. You'd have to drive all day, for eight hours, five days a week, to run up the miles that would get you to the $600 mileage allowance, if you were getting the IRS standard at that time of 55 cents per mile.

When Hugo Rojas was elected to the board, he wanted to upgrade his ride. He picked out a BMW sports sedan that he could lease for $600 a month. Of course, he could not do that, since his sole source of income, teaching karate, would not allow him to pay $600 a month for a car. But days after his election, one of the attorneys who were helping his election asked me to write a letter vouching for Rojas' income stream of $600 a month for his vehicle allowance.

With that letter in hand, Rojas got his BMW, and that was the vehicle he drove to the board meeting the night he led the revolt that led to my departure. He was still driving it, but had to find another way to pay the $600 monthly lease payment.

You might say I was axed over $600 a month for each of the board members. But my contract was not renewed for a lot of reasons besides that. Among them was my failure to learn the most important lessons I should have learned from Jose Fernandez – how to coddle and care for the elected board members.

Towards the end of my time as Interim, and with the board settling on a permanent Supe in Gregory O'Brien, I proposed an extension of two years for the three assistant supes who had steered the district during the crisis, Allan Mucerino, Ron Hacker and, myself.

But in a classic case of misreading the tea leaves, I put it on the agenda without whispering sweet nothings in the ears of each board member to assure their votes. I also put it on the agenda for one of the few board meetings I would ever miss, while in Florida for a week to watch my daughter pitch for her college softball team.

Rojas got his revenge for the reduction of the $600 car allowance (it was now $200) on a night when I was 3,000 miles away. He and the other board members approved contracts for Mucerino and Hacker, but declined to approve mine by a 3-2 vote. It was early March, and I knew I was going to be leaving CV when my contract expired on July 1.

There were a few last-gasp options available to me and the new supe, O'Brien. But all involved Rojas changing his mind and voting to extend my contract as Assistant Supe of H.R. and Hugo Rojas was nothing if not capable of holding a grudge.

Some would suggest the end was written for me the day I took the Interim job. That's often the case in educational administration and I should have known as much.

After a couple of months of consideration, I realized the best move was the easiest. I was going to retire when my contract expired. I had never planned to retire at the age of 67 – or any other number for that matter – but that was where it was going to play out.

Three months after my retirement, Fernandez was arrested on a raft of bribery and misappropriation of funds charges. He spent Labor Day Weekend in jail, and I was in the courtroom in Torrance when he was arraigned. Three years later, I testified in his preliminary hearing when he was bound over for trial. That trial was among the many postponed in spring of 2020 by the coronavirus pandemic.

Although I felt there was unfinished business that I could have addressed at CV, I left with my head held high. I had made it a better district than it was when I arrived, by a large measure. I left a high-performing H.R. department, and a legacy of excellent administrators at all of the schools and a number of great young teachers.

THAT'S -30- (2020)

During most of my three decades in journalism, the accepted way to end a story was -30-.

Yet I'm having trouble putting a -30- on this collection of memoirs, mostly because it remains a work in progress. I realize that actuarial tables would suggest I'm on the last lap or two of my journey, yet I'm not ready to concede anything.

When I left active employment as Assistant Superintendent of Human Resources for the Centinela Valley Union High School District, I wasn't ready to talk about my working life in the past tense.

I was retiring, mostly because my contract had come to an end, and during my time as Interim Superintendent, I wasn't politically astute enough to manipulate a board vote on renewing my contract as Assistant Supe. I missed the signs that a grudge-holding board president was going to hold me to blame for the reduction in his monthly car allowance.

During 7-plus years at CVUHSD, I learned a graduate degree worth of knowledge about the governance of a school district. For 50 years, newspaper and education careers combined, I said I wasn't a politician and I didn't play political games. I left those tactics to those who protected me, the sports editors or superintendents who knew how to manipulate the tender egos of those in true power.

It's fair to say my retirement, at age 67, was my own fault, I still had a lot to offer, and incoming superintendent, Greg O'Brien, cried on a couple

223

of occasions when he realized he could not keep me as part of his staff. Maybe he was just being emotional, or maybe he actually thought I was an important member of the team going forward.

But once the final score was entered into the scoreboard, 3-2 against renewing me, it was time to accept the outcome.

On the day I stopped going to work for the first time in more than 50 years, July 1, 2015, I went to the gym as I did every day. I didn't talk much about my new reality. Just pushed through my workout, then came home and faced the first day of the rest of my life: What now? It was 7:30 a.m., I had worked out, eaten breakfast, read two newspapers, and didn't have a plan for the rest of the day. Or the rest of my life.

That set me on a frenzy of household tasks that had been on the back burner for years. Things like getting the house painted. Things like starting an autobiography.

Not surprisingly, the house was painted in a hurry because I was using some of my retirement largess to pay for it. The book was officially started, but my work on that was fitful for the next couple of years. I would write a chapter, then lose motivation.

The guy who writes up weekly agendas and makes notes on a scratch pad on his desk was still looking for direction.

Two months after my retirement date, I found a Mediterranean cruise for Nancy and me to take, starting in Rome and including Barcelona and Monte Carlo among other attractive stops.

We decided that cruising was definitely a great way to vacation, and have taken at least one cruise (sometimes two) every year since. Only in 2020, the year of the Corona-virus pandemic, did we skip our cruise. We had been planning to fly to Amsterdam and cruise around Norway. That's one we'll just push back for a year.

Nancy remains busy working – she's 10 years younger – so I was able to spend a lot of time chatting with Eve and Dexter on our twice-daily walks. Nancy has been working for a registry, which allows her to tailor her work schedule. Ideally, she'll work 40 weeks in most years, although that won't happen this year.

Allan Mucerino, who lost out on the CVUHSD superintendency because of board incompetence, was quickly snapped up to shepherd the fortunes of the Duarte USD. He was as ready for a superintendency as anyone in Southern California. Within six months, he had hired me as a consultant, and I worked on a number of H.R. projects in Duarte. I was also available as a mentor to the principal who took his first H.R. job in that district.

This was a positive, and I worked pretty consistently in Duarte for a couple of years, before the frequency of projects began to diminish. After four years, Mucerino moved to another district. We remain in touch, but there have been no needs for a consultant. The Duarte experience was a great way to ease myself onto the sidelines.

I was working as a "coach," which is what Moose had always called me when we worked together, and that was enjoyable.

Gradually, my working focus was changing, and I was becoming engaged as a softball umpire. I was working 30 to 50 games a year at the high school level, including a couple of CIF semifinal and quarterfinal assignments. I was also working rec ball at the age group level, doing as many as 150 games a year, including district and state tournaments.

I threw myself into umpiring, much as I had journalism, coaching softball, teaching and school district administration. I remain that focused individual who keeps working to get better. I think it's safe to say that won't change. My most immediate goal is to reach the level where I am nominated for a national tournament by USA Softball. It's a lofty goal, but seems within reach.

Nancy and I are also enjoying watching Randy and Allie grow into their adult lives. Randy and wife Sylvie have daughter Geneva, who Nancy (call her Nana) just adores and goes to visit in Phoenix whenever possible.

Also in Phoenix, daughter Allison (Allie), has just finished her second of four years toward her doctorate in veterinary medicine at Midwestern University. When she finished Wheaton with a degree in biochemistry, the common wisdom was that it would take a year to get accepted into a DVM program, but that only stoked her competitive juices. No gap year for the girl who loved to throw a slow curve over the outside corner on a 3-2 count.

Both kids are proficient skiers, and our last vacation before the Pandemic was a family skiing trip to Salt Lake City. I can still make turns with both of these athletic offspring, but I'll also live vicariously when they take off down a challenging line in the *off-piste* areas.

Whatever remains before -30- becomes official will include living more vicariously than actively, although I'm going to hold off on that as long as possible. Today's plan gives you an idea how I am handling that: After stretching, breakfast and reading two newspapers, I'll go out for an hour or 75 minutes with the dogs; then I'll devote two hours to this writing project; then ride my bike for an hour and a half; then lunch and a brief nap, followed by a 45-minute walk with the dogs.

I'm also reading a minimum of one book a week, and will throw myself back into watching baseball and the Dodgers when that's allowed.

Life remains a very active sport for me, and that won't change as long as I'm calling the shots.

Bob Cox
Summer 2020

Special Thanks

I have known Dan McLean for more than 50 years, as a colleague, volleyball partner, co-coach and friend. He has always been one of the most meticulous copy editors on the sports or news desks. His diligence in finding the errors large and small have helped me move this project forward. Any errors that remain are mine, solely. Dan did all he could to help.

Bob's Jobs

1960-62
Delivered *Idaho Free Press* (Nampa, Idaho) on bicycle

1960-62
Farm work, picked strawberries, weeded alfalfa fields, bucked hay bails

1963-64
Delivered *L.A. Times* (early morning car route); Kitchen assistant, dishwasher, cafeteria at Culver City Memorial Hospital (now Brotman Memorial)

1964-Jan. 1968
Hollywood Citizen-News, part-time sports writer, leading up to fulltime work in summer and fall of 1965

Jan 1968-March 1970
U.S. Navy Reserve Active Duty, Fort Harrison, Indiana, then Naval Air Station, Atsugi, Japan

April-August 1970
Hollywood Citizen-News, assistant sports editor, news editor, managing editor

December 1970-May 1998
The Daily Breeze, sports writer; plus part-time and free-lance work for The Associated Press, Sports Illustrated, The Sporting News, Pro Football Weekly, and other publications.

July 1998-January 2008
Teacher 5 years at Caroldale Learning Community (4th-5th combo, 4th Grade, Middle School); then Teacher Advisor, Specialist, and Assistant Director (Recruitment), LAUSD downtown L.A

Summer 1999-2002
Various jobs in training new teachers with Teach in L.A. (L.A. Teaching Fellows), and LAUSD District Intern Program

January 2008-July 1, 2015
Assistant Superintendent, Centinela Valley Union High School District, Interim Superintendent last year, Lawndale, CA.

August 2015-Present
Occasional consulting with Duarte **Unified School District**

2010-Present
Umpire, high school and USA Softball recreation and travel ball.